INTRODUCTION

S EPTEMBER 11, 2001, was a day of untold tragedy for America—a day of enormous grief and terror for many, and at the least, a day of horror and disruption for all of us. Most of us experienced inconvenience as airplanes were grounded and offices, schools, and businesses were temporarily closed; and all of us came face to face with the very real possibility of future disasters.

What might happen to you, to your family, to your community the next time disaster strikes—whether it's another terrorist attack, flood, or famine? What if your livelihood were cut off? Could you provide for your family without an income? What if you're denied access to the consumer goods you take for granted—food, clothing, medicine? What if the banks, grocery stores, and restaurants were to close, or you were unable to reach them? What if no medical services were available and utilities such as electricity, gas, water, and telephone shut down?

Are you prepared?

Indeed, few of us would find it easy—if possible—to provide for our families in crisis situations if we had only ourselves on which to depend. That's why many people choose to be prepared to care for themselves and their families whatever the future may bring, to prepare to sustain a provident future even in times of crisis and overwhelming need. The phrase "provident living" means being wise, frugal, prudent, and making preparation for the future while living life today and taking care of immediate needs. In other words, those who enjoy provident living are able to *provide* for the future.

How can you prepare to provide for whatever your future might hold? The answer is through *emergency home storage*. The term *home storage* is defined as any item purchased for future use and stored in the home. This can be food, water, clothing, and bedding; emergency supplies; medical kits; equipment or fuel for cooking, heating, or lighting. The more specific term, *food storage,* is defined as storing food that is not needed immediately and could be used at a later time. This includes commercial or home-canned or bottled foods; vegetables and fruit from the garden or orchard; dry grain, rice, many types of beans, and dehydrated foods. The way to prepare is to stock your own home grocery store with exactly what your family likes and rotate the items by using the older ones first as you replenish with fresh items so you never run out—not even if you were unable to buy food for several months, or even an entire year.

Some church organizations recommend that their members have a one-year supply of food, water, cash, clothing, and fuel. I recommend that you keep an emergency supply that will last at least three months in your home grocery store, eventually expand that to a six-month supply, and work toward a year's supply, which will enable you to see through almost any crisis that could come your way.

Why Be Prepared?

As a consultant on home storage, I encounter many parents who are motivated to store food and other necessities for emergencies by the thought of hearing their children crying from fear, darkness, cold, and hunger. Parents have the enormous responsibility of providing for and taking care of their children's needs. Those who store food find that having adequate food and emergency supplies on hand brings them peace of mind and enables them to rest easy, knowing their children will be taken care of even if disaster were to strike.

Do you have such peace of mind?

There are many reasons for storing a well-rounded supply of emergency food, water, cash, clothing, and fuel. The natural and man-made disasters that we continually read and hear about through news services should serve to remind us that we need to be better prepared personally, as families, and as communities.

Disaster can strike in the form of national recession, international terrorism or war, or a force of nature such as earthquake, hurricane, tornado, or even volcanic eruption. It can also be a personal situation, such as accident, illness, death, bankruptcy, job layoff, or simply a period when a cash shortage threatens financial devastation. Or it may strike other family members, friends, or even strangers in our own or the world community who face a crisis. Perhaps a hurricane or earthquake will take its toll on lives and leave many survivors homeless and starving. Without the help from nearby communities that bring food and provisions, people experiencing such disasters may well starve. Although we certainly hope we do not become victims of any disasters such as those mentioned, we must be prepared for the possibility. Being prepared will give us many advantages, including the following:

Self-Sufficiency. In times of recession, large companies often announce job layoffs, which may leave thousands of people without paychecks. If you were to be among those laid off—but you have a reserve of food, cash, clothing, and fuel—you would be able to get through the lean times and not have to ask for help.

Ability to Help Others. If you are prepared, then rather than being dependent on others to help you, you can be the one to help others who are in need.

Peace of Mind. If you are prepared, then you will not fear.

That is what this book is about: being prepared for an emergency. Whether the emergency lasts for a brief or an extended period of time, knowing that you are prepared to face it will bring peace of mind and put you in a position to help others rather than being the one who must ask for help.

How Can You Be Prepared?

We as a nation rely almost totally on grocery stores, delis, and restaurants for food. Yet if you were to ask a grocery store manager to tell you how long it would take to empty the shelves in a grocery store in the event of a crisis, the answer would be approximately two to three days; they just don't keep that much on hand. People facing the threat of a shortage tend to panic and storm the grocery stores to buy anything they can get. And if there were a trucking problem, those shelves may not be filled again until the problem finally subsides.

Should famine, natural disaster, terrorist attack, or economic calamity prevent us from buying food in the grocery stores, we should be prepared to handle these emergencies ourselves. However, households in general seldom have more than a one-week supply of ingredients with which to make meals. If you had to live on what you have in your pantry for an extended period of time, you would soon wish that you had a well-rounded supply of nutritious and good-tasting food.

That's why I recommend you stock your own home grocery store with a well-balanced supply of foods that includes all the ingredients you need to make your family's favorite meals for three months. Once you've gathered that amount, I recommend you then expand your storage to grains, beans, rice, soups, bread-making ingredients, spices, condiments, fun foods, and dehydrated foods that could sustain your family for as long as a year.

Where, you might ask, could I possibly keep that much food?

I believe you have such a place in your home—whether a pantry, basement, spare bedroom, closet, junk room, space under the stairway, or garage—and I suggest that you go to work transforming it into your own home grocery store and pharmacy. Somehow you'll get shelves in there—by building them, having them built, or buying them pre-built. It's certainly doable, as many provident, forward-looking families can attest.

Most Americans carry insurance for their business, house, car, health, and life. Home storage is insurance that you will be prepared for an emergency. It makes a lot of sense to me, and I sleep better at night knowing that my family is prepared. That's why I recommend that you, too, begin storing food for emergency use, and the reason I wrote this book.

What's in This Book?

Emergency Food Storage & Survival Handbook provides the information you need to prepare and implement an emergency food storage and survival plan to ensure that your family will enjoy provident living. Chapter 1 provides the basics of preparing for short-term emergencies so you will know what to do and be ready to grab what you need at a moment's notice. You'll also learn about alternatives to the communication, sanitation, and utility systems you currently rely on, so you can retain your personal health and hygiene and have continued access to light, heat, power, and fuel.

Chapter 2 focuses on water, the most basic necessity for survival, explaining why you should store water, as well as how and how much of it you should store. Chapter 3 explores the economics of emergency storage and shows how practical planning can enable you to become self-sufficient, save money, and avoid waste.

In chapter 4, you'll find ideas on where you might best locate your home grocery store and pharmacy, how to properly prepare and maintain your inventory to prevent spoilage and deterioration, and how to ready your store for "business."

Chapter 5 discusses the surprising array of foods that are suitable for storage, as well as some non-food items that you'll need to retain your quality of life.

By reading chapter 6, you'll get ideas on various ways you might obtain the items to stock your store—via thrifty purchasing, through growing your own food and sprouting seeds, and by doing your own dehydrating and canning.

Chapter 7, "Implementing Your Food Storage Program," pulls it all together and provides a plan of action tailored to your family's needs. It further divides the daunting task of stocking your store into ten clear steps that you can tackle one at a time. You'll also learn how to maintain your emergency food store by tracking and effectively rotating inventory.

Chapter 8 offers many nutritious and delicious recipes that are composed of ingredients that can be stored long term. You'll find that your family can enjoy not only tasty beans and grains, but hearty soups, casseroles, and even desserts that will not only sustain but provide you with nourishment and eating pleasure. I have given information on substituting dried products for fresh in most of the recipes and have included charts for reconstituting these products. Finally, in the Resource Guide at the end of the book, you'll find a host of resources for further information as well as supplies that can help guarantee the success of your emergency food storage and survival.

By reading *Emergency Food Storage & Survival Handbook,* you are taking your first step toward being prepared for anything your future may bring. By following the guidelines detailed on the pages ahead, you can soon enjoy the peace of mind that is part of provident living.

CHAPTER 1

Preparing for Short-Term Emergencies

B EING PREPARED for any type of emergency is part of provident living. You can start by thinking about the most likely disasters that could happen in your area, and plan what you would do in case of various emergencies. Planning will help your family get organized and feel more secure. Although you can't anticipate exactly what you might encounter in your future, you do have a pretty good idea of what items your family needs for daily living and what you find useful in case of illness and injury, and you might even think about what the typical backpacker needs to take for a three-day wilderness survival trip. Since short-term emergencies are not only the most common, but the easiest to plan for, we'll start by preparing for those.

I define short-term emergencies as those that last anywhere from a few hours to a few days. Sometimes we have warning and time to get ourselves ready to deal with the crisis. For example, you may know ahead of time that your water will be shut off. You can wash clothes, take showers, water the lawn, as well as fill containers and bathtubs in anticipation of the shortage to minimize the inconvenience. Real crises, however, seldom provide enough warning to enable you to prepare, thus you must quickly decide what to do and scramble to put together what you need— or do without. By anticipating what you might need in a crisis, you can determine in advance just what your family will do, as well as have all the items you need for emergency survival ready to use. The pages that follow provide suggestions to help you plan and prepare.

Prepare an Evacuation Plan

If a disaster such as a fire, flood, or chemical spill is heading toward your home, it's best to evacuate while you still have time. You may, in fact, be ordered to do so. Therefore, having a plan for emergency evacuation is essential. Each member of the family should know exactly what to do.

Decide on a meeting place if you must evacuate quickly. Know ahead of time what you need to take with you, and have those items packed in your "72-hour kit" (as described later) and stashed in a convenient location so you can quickly grab them on your way out the door. Leave a note in a place where it can be easily seen to let absent family members or others who might come looking for you know where you are going.

In the event of a crisis such as an earthquake or tornado, decide ahead of time which family member you will contact to let everyone know you are safe. Choose someone living in a different town or state who would not be involved in a local disaster. Call, or otherwise try to get a message through, to let that person know that you have evacuated safely and where you are headed. If everyone in the family knows whom to call, it will be less confusing, especially if anyone was away from home when you had to evacuate.

Have a Car Kit Ready

A friend and I once got stranded on a freeway in the middle of the night. To get help, we had to walk about a mile in extreme cold, with only a very weak flashlight to find our way. This frightening experience prompted me to get a car kit and be prepared in case it ever happened again.

Having such a kit filled and stashed in your car at all times will give you peace of mind every time you drive your car since breakdowns and accidents can occur at any moment. In addition, your kit could prove invaluable should you need to evacuate by car or even use your car for temporary shelter.

You can either put together a car kit with items you already have at home or purchase a premade kit (see figure 1.1).

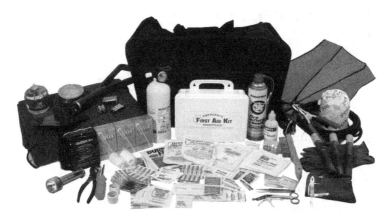

(Photo courtesy of Emergency Essentials)

Figure 1.1   Premade emergency car kit.

Sample Emergency Car Kit

- ❏ 3-day supply of water
- ❏ 3-day supply of emergency food and snacks
- ❏ Lightweight wool blanket or emergency reflective blanket
- ❏ Hats and gloves
- ❏ Extra clothing
- ❏ Hand and body warmers
- ❏ Waterproof ponchos
- ❏ Flashlight with extra batteries
- ❏ Waterproof matches and butane lighter
- ❏ Road flares or light sticks
- ❏ 100-hour candle
- ❏ Reflectors
- ❏ Gas can with extra gas
- ❏ Cans of oil
- ❏ Jumper cables
- ❏ Jack and lug wrench
- ❏ Tire pump or Fix-a-Flat
- ❏ Tire chains
- ❏ Tow chain
- ❏ Basic tools and a small shovel
- ❏ Ice scraper
- ❏ Extra fan belt, radiator hose, and fuses
- ❏ Small first-aid kit
- ❏ Multipurpose knife
- ❏ Toilet paper
- ❏ Emergency money ($20 in small bills and coins)
- ❏ Other _____

Plan for Emergency Shelter

If you were evacuated for a few days and had to sleep outdoors in the winter, could you do it? The Scouts do! They know how to build snow caves similar to igloos into a hillside or use waterproof tents that stay nice and warm even in freezing temperatures.

Your family might want to practice this extreme survival skill in the middle of winter to see just how prepared you really are. The following items are very important for a warm, waterproof shelter.

Emergency Shelter Needs

- ❑ Large tent with repair kit
- ❑ 25' × 60' plastic sheeting (4-millimeter thickness)
- ❑ 10' × 12' plastic tarp (waterproof)
- ❑ 150' cording or rope
- ❑ Hammer
- ❑ Pocketknife
- ❑ Duct tape

Prepare a 72-Hour Emergency Kit

During many types of disasters, people are often ordered to evacuate their homes quickly. They may have to live in temporary quarters such as at a public school or another emergency evacuation site. If this were to happen to you, you may only have a minute or two to grab your belongings and go. You certainly wouldn't have time to think very seriously about what you would need. That's why it's important for you to carefully consider and list the items you'd find essential in any crisis situation, prepare "72-hour kits" that include those items for each family member, and store the kits where you can get to them quickly and easily.

A 72-hour emergency kit is designed to contain the items that you would need to survive for a three-day period. Even when a crisis situation lasts longer than three days, 72 hours is approximately how long it takes to get help after a disaster hits. Each family member should have his or her own kit, tailored to the individual's specific needs.

You can purchase a premade 72-hour kit with a lot of great products in it, such as shown in figure 1.2, or you can make your own kit by assembling the items you already have at home that would be most helpful in an emergency. It's just a matter of collecting them into a suitcase or backpack. To decide what you should include, ask yourself questions such as these:

If there were an emergency situation in my community and we are left without water, lights, and heat, what would I need to survive in my home or elsewhere?

What would I need to cook and stay warm?

If I were forced to evacuate my home, what personal items would I need to take with me?

Write your list. Keep in mind that your kit must be easy to carry and lightweight in case you must walk to a safe destination.

The following list is to give you ideas. Remember, you must tailor each 72-hour kit for the individual. Again, having a 72-hour kit ready for each member of your family will give you a great deal of peace of mind.

Sample 72-Hour Kit

- [ ] Backpack or suitcase (in which to put kit items)
- [ ] Tube-tent shelter or lightweight tent
- [ ] 15' nylon cord

Figure 1.2   Premade emergency 72-hour kit.

❑ Battery-powered radio (with extra batteries)

❑ Sleeping bag or lightweight wool blanket

❑ Space blanket

❑ Flashlight with batteries

❑ Emergency light source or light stick

❑ Candles

❑ Waterproof matches and butane lighter

❑ Whistle

❑ Pocketknife

❑ Small first-aid kit

❑ Personal medication (extra supply)

❑ Personal sanitary items

❑ Wet towelettes

- ❏ Toilet paper
- ❏ 2 garbage bags (30-gallon size)
- ❏ Warm socks and clothing
- ❏ Lightweight poncho
- ❏ Leather gloves and hat
- ❏ Hand warmers
- ❏ Water (bottles or pouches)
- ❏ Water purification tablets
- ❏ Ready-to-eat food (nonperishable, lightweight, 3-day supply)
- ❏ Hard candy
- ❏ Can opener (if needed)
- ❏ Paper plates and cups and plastic utensils
- ❏ Small cook stove with fuel
- ❏ Pens and small notebook
- ❏ Money in small bills and coins ($200 or more)
- ❏ Other _____

The hardest item to carry is water because of its weight. Purified water pouches are available and easy to carry in a backpack (12 per person), or a plastic bottle full of water can be easily carried (the two-liter soda bottles are best for packing).

Space blankets are lightweight and will keep you warm. A light wool blanket is also very nice.

Considering Special Family Members

Keep in mind that what you put in each pack will vary with the individual. Some family members—particularly the oldest and youngest—will require special consideration.

The Elderly

If you have an elderly person in your household, his or her special needs must be taken into consideration. If this individual needs medications, I suggest that you keep an emergency supply of medication on hand just in case you could not get to a pharmacy or a doctor. Prepare a 72-hour kit that meets this person's special needs.

Babies and Young Children

If your family includes a baby or young children, meeting their needs during a crisis should be a top priority. Children, even babies, can feel their parents' stress. If your little ones are afraid, your words or actions can calm them down and reassure them that everything is all right. It will be easier for you to be reassuring if you have everything ready for your children, including special "comfort" foods, toys, and blankets.

The following is a list of items you'll need to collect for a 72-hour kit (or longer-term emergency storage) for your baby.

Sample 72-Hour Kit for Baby

- ❏ Disposable diapers
- ❏ Wet towelettes
- ❏ Baby lotion and diaper rash ointment
- ❏ Garbage bags for used diapers
- ❏ Blanket and extra clothing
- ❏ Baby formula
- ❏ Evaporated whole milk
- ❏ Powdered milk
- ❏ Karo syrup
- ❏ Bottles with nipples

- ❏ Baby food and juices
- ❏ Spoons (plastic)
- ❏ Medications
- ❏ Toys
- ❏ Other _____

An infant who is nursing may not require additional foods, as long as the mother continues to get sufficient nourishment. If the mother is unable to nurse, however, evaporated whole milk mixed with Karo syrup can be used as a formula. For babies already on solids, it is not necessary to store large quantities of commercial baby foods. Once infants can eat solid foods, they should be able to eat the foods the rest of the family is eating. The foods may need to be mashed or thinned with milk.

Until the age of two, a child who is weaned from the breast needs the fats best provided by whole milk. Therefore, if you have a toddler, you should store some evaporated whole milk that you could add to nonfat dry milk that has been reconstituted.

If your child has an allergy to cow's milk, then a cereal-based formula may be used. If your child needs special types of food, plan for this and stock up on them.

Following are suggestions for additional items to include in a small child's 72-hour kit.

Sample 72-Hour Kit Extras for Children

- ❏ Books
- ❏ Games or puzzles
- ❏ Coloring books and crayons
- ❏ Small stuffed animals and toys
- ❏ Comfort foods
- ❏ Other _____

First-Aid Medical Kit

A standard first-aid kit is very important for emergencies. It is better if your kit is waterproof; otherwise, keep all items in sealable plastic bags to keep moisture out. Store your first-aid kit in an easily accessible area of your home or garage. You can purchase a premade kit (see figure 1.3) or create one of your own by collecting the following items and putting them into a small suitcase or box.

Sample First-Aid Kit

- [ ] First-aid book
- [ ] Essential personal medications
- [ ] Cold and cough medicine
- [ ] Ibuprofen, acetaminophen, aspirin

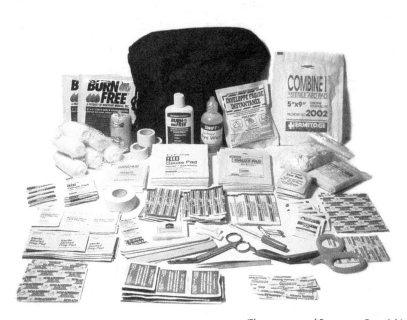

(Photo courtesy of Emergency Essentials)

Figure 1.3 First-aid kit.

A Safe Room

A safe room is the spot in your house that would be the safest place for you to go if you needed to quickly take shelter because of a bomb attack, tornado, hurricane, or any other disaster. You have probably seen movies in which people take cover from a tornado in an underground root cellar and emerge unharmed when it's over. Your safe room is similar to that root cellar or to a bomb shelter.

Choose a room in your basement (if you have one) or inside the house or garage that you can seal off with plastic and duct tape. Cover all the windows and vents, and seal off door jambs and floor boards to protect your family from contaminants that may seep in.

Think through every aspect—food, water, warmth, communication, sanitation, ventilation, medical supplies, and even entertainment. (Check with your local bookstore to find complete information on creating a safe room.)

- ☐ Antacid
- ☐ Syrup of ipecac
- ☐ Powdered antibiotic
- ☐ Antibiotic ointment
- ☐ Rubbing alcohol
- ☐ Hydrogen peroxide
- ☐ Laxative and diarrhea remedy
- ☐ Antihistamine

Equip your safe room with everything that would sustain your family for up to two weeks. It would probably be best to stock your safe room with cans of food that you can open and eat cold right out of the can. Don't forget the can opener!

Be sure to have a radio and at least a two-week supply of fresh batteries on hand (plan to use and replace your safe room batteries so they don't expire). If you were involved in a bombing and could not leave your safe room, the radio would be your link to the outside world.

This safe room would be a good place to store the items that you have been collecting for emergencies. Remember to include warm hats, gloves, wool socks, coats, extra clothing, and such.

If an emergency should occur, grab your 72-hour kits from the closet, garage, or wherever they're stashed, and head for the safe room.

❑ Sunblock and lip balm
❑ Instant cold and hot packs
❑ Elastic bandages (2 or more)
❑ Triangular bandages
❑ Adhesive bandages of all sizes (100 count)
❑ Butterfly closures
❑ Assorted sterile gauze pads
❑ First-aid tape

- ❑ Cotton balls and swabs
- ❑ Small scissors
- ❑ Tweezers
- ❑ Thermometer
- ❑ Sanitary napkins
- ❑ Small splints (Popsicle sticks or tongue depressors)
- ❑ Waterproof matches
- ❑ Plastic spoons
- ❑ Safety pins
- ❑ Needle and thread
- ❑ Pocketknife
- ❑ Flashlight (with batteries)
- ❑ Lightweight blanket or space blanket
- ❑ Other _____

Personal Medications

It's very important that you include personal medications in your medical kit as well as in your 72-hour kit. If you have to evacuate quickly and don't have your mandatory medication, it could mean life or death. People who depend on certain medications often cannot miss more than three days of medication without suffering severe consequences. Talk with your doctor and explain that you need an emergency supply of medication that you can keep with your 72-hour kit and medical kit. Medications that expire within a few months will need to be rotated. Painkillers, such as acetaminophen (Tylenol) and aspirin, and powdered antibiotics are good for everyone to have on hand.

Plan for Emergency Communication

If the power goes out or you have to evacuate, a crucial item to have is a portable radio and good batteries. In times of crisis, the emergency broadcasting system gives warnings and information that are vital to each community. The following list of items for communication can be very helpful in an emergency:

Emergency Communication Needs

- ❏ Portable radio and extra batteries
- ❏ Solar-powered battery charger and rechargeable batteries
- ❏ Cell phone
- ❏ Walkie-talkies
- ❏ Ham radio
- ❏ Flares
- ❏ Flashlight with extra batteries (for signaling as well as light)
- ❏ Extra bulbs for the flashlight
- ❏ Battery-powered spotlight
- ❏ Other _____

Prepare for Emergency Sanitation

Those of us who are accustomed to using full bathroom facilities, laundry appliances, and a kitchen sink or dishwasher will find it a challenge to keep clean during a crisis. In addition, sanitation is particularly important in case of a flood or earthquake, for example—especially if a family member is injured. To maintain adequate sanitation, you should prepare a "sanitation kit" and have on hand the supplies necessary for keeping yourself, your clothes, and your dishes clean.

Sanitation Kit

This kit, which the entire family will share, can be put into a five-gallon bucket and stored along with your 72-hour kits. The bucket can be used as a toilet if necessary (see figure 1.4). You can even purchase a screw-on lid that fits over the bucket and has a toilet

(Photo courtesy of Frontier Survival)

Figure 1.4 Five-gallon bucket with screw-on toilet seat lid.

PREPARING FOR SHORT-TERM EMERGENCIES

seat on top of it. See the Resource Guide in the back of the book for such supplies.

Sample Emergency Sanitation Kit

❏ Five-gallon bucket
❏ Toilet seat lid (screw-on type)
❏ Plastic garbage bags (to fit the 5-gallon bucket)
❏ Toilet paper
❏ Disinfectants and bleach
❏ Washboard and tub
❏ Clothesline or rack
❏ Laundry soap
❏ Hand soap and antibacterial soap
❏ Paper towels or hand towels
❏ Toothbrushes and toothpaste
❏ Personal hygiene and feminine products
❏ Lots of water for washing hands, clothes, and dishes
❏ Other _____

Portable toilets, such as Porta-potties, and composting toilets are also available for purchase. They are expensive, but require no plumbing and are self-contained. The composting toilet turns human waste into compost.

If you live in an area where you have a little extra space on your property, an outhouse can be constructed by digging a pit about three feet deep; installing a wooden box, with a toilet-seat-shaped hole cut out, over the pit; and erecting a small shed-type enclosure around it. To release odor from the outhouse, you can vent it by inserting a 2-inch diameter plastic pipe through the roof and down into the wooden box. A cut-out "crescent moon" or other shape in the door will also help with air flow. If you haven't the time or materials to build an outhouse enclosure, you can create privacy by hanging a curtain around the pit. Attach the curtain to nearby trees or to metal stakes or PVC pipe pounded into the ground.

Bathing Needs

We live in a world of conveniences and would have to make a major lifestyle change to live without clean running water. There's no doubt that we'd miss our regular showers and baths, but you can learn to stay clean when water is in extremely short supply. Sponge bathing is probably the best way to conserve water. Heat up the water, lather up a cloth or sponge with soap, and sponge it on. Rinse off all the soap with clean water and a clean cloth, then dry off with a towel.

Washing and Drying Clothing

During an emergency, washing clothes may have to be postponed or done the old-fashioned way—by hand in a small amount of water. Heat water in a large pot and put a small amount of laundry soap in the wash water. Wash garments by hand and rinse in another pot of clean hot water. Hang clothes up on a clothesline or somewhere in the house where they will dry.

Washing Dishes

Store paper plates and cups for use during short-term emergencies so you won't have to worry about washing dishes. You can also eat from cans and packages to avoid doing dishes. However, because this is expensive and results in unnecessary waste, using paper products is not practical for periods longer than a few days. When you use dishes or cook with pots and pans (which is necessary even when you use paper plates), they will have to be washed by hand. To wash dishes, heat water in a large pot. Divide it into two large bowls which hold the wash and rinse water. Be sure to store dish soap and paper towels.

Emergency Utilities and Fuel

Imagine what you would need if your power, lights, and heat went out for more than a few hours. We all know the inconvenience of brief outages, especially when they occur after dark or when we're cooking dinner. And we've read newspaper accounts of people who freeze to death when they are without heat during a cold spell. We can well imagine the longer-term effects of being deprived of some of the utilities on which we depend.

Electrical Outages

When our electrical supply goes out, almost all of us lose the use of our lights as well as most appliances. The following is a list of items you would need to have on hand for illumination.

Emergency Lighting Needs

- ❏ Flashlights and batteries
- ❏ Flashlight bulbs
- ❏ Gas or kerosene lantern and fuel (with extra mantles)
- ❏ Waterproof matches and regular wooden matches
- ❏ Candles with holders
- ❏ Liquid paraffin or 100-hour candles
- ❏ Butane igniter or cigarette lighter
- ❏ Other _____

Using an Emergency Generator

Generators are an alternative source of power for short-term emergencies. They can be used as a backup source to your overall power supply or to keep a single or selective appliances or circuits working. Generators, however, are expensive pieces of equipment and require a lot of fuel to run, making them an impractical alternative power source for extended outages. Storing the fuel required to run a generator is a problem as well.

Salvaging Food from Your Refrigerator and Freezer

What should you do about the refrigerator and freezer if your electricity goes off?

If your freezer is loaded with food and the power goes out, your food will keep just fine for several hours if you don't open the freezer door. If the power is off for an extended period of time (more than 12 hours, for example), you'll need to take action to salvage the food. If this happens in winter when temperatures are below or near freezing, you can pack the frozen food in large coolers or other containers and temporarily store it outside or in your garage for weeks, or even months, if temperatures remain frigid. Otherwise, quickly take newspaper or freezer paper and wrap the food with a thick layer of paper. You can put several items together and stuff any spaces between items with wadded up newspaper to help maintain the cold to keep the food frozen longer. Return all packed items to your freezer, and then keep the door shut until the power comes back on. You can add additional insulation around the door of the freezer (preferably insulation pads or blankets, though even newspaper will help some) and tape or hold it in place with a rope or bungee cord to help keep in the cold. The food should stay frozen for up to two or three days if the door isn't opened again.

Once the power comes back on, meat can be refrozen if it is still partially frozen with ice crystals. Once the meat has thawed out, however, it needs to be cooked and eaten, canned, dehydrated, or made into jerky.

You can use a generator to keep your freezer going in an emergency. However, it uses a lot of fuel and may not be worthwhile as a long-term solution, but it will buy you some time to figure out a more practical solution to your thawing problem.

The food inside your refrigerator will be safe for a few hours, depending on the temperature of the room in which it's located and on how much it's opened during the electrical outage. When the food inside the refrigerator reaches room temperature, it will spoil quickly. Eat what you can, and when in doubt, throw it out. If the outage happens in the winter and your outdoor air is near or below refrigeration temperature, you can keep the food in coolers or boxes outside. If temperatures are below freezing, cover the coolers or boxes with blankets to insulate them so they don't freeze.

Once your power comes back on, clean out your refrigerator and freezer just in case bacteria have started to grow. Use a disinfectant soap to wash the refrigerator and rinse with a mixture of hot water and bleach. (One-half cup of bleach to one cup of water will kill the bacteria.)

Cooking Alternatives

There are many ways to cook when an emergency prevents you from using your stove, oven, and even your microwave, Crock-Pot, or other electrical appliances. Maybe you have a camp stove in your garage, a charcoal barbecue grill on your deck, or a fireplace in your home.

When you can't use your stove or oven, whether electric or gas, you can do fine for a while on fresh, canned, or dehydrated foods that don't require cooking. Tuna and many other canned foods can be opened and eaten right out of the can. Sooner or later, though, you'll want an alternative. You might start by imagining how people cooked before they had modern-day appliances.

For hundreds of years, people cooked over fires or on woodstoves without any electricity or gas. We need to take lessons from our pioneer ancestors, who used cast-iron kettles hung over an open fire. You, too, can make soups and stews, potato dishes, meat dishes, breads, and a lot of other foods in such kettles, commonly called Dutch ovens, which you can use over open fires or on top of woodstoves (see figure 1.5).

Woodstoves

Most of our ancestors used old-fashioned woodstoves as their primary source of cooking, baking, and warmth. Although "heat" stoves or woodstove "inserts" are pretty common these days, the so-called "cookstoves," which use wood as their fuel source, are quite rare and need chimneys or some sort of outdoor ventilation when used indoors.

Dutch Ovens

Cooking in a Dutch oven is one of the best ways to cook outdoors (see figure 1.5). You can use charcoal briquettes or wood to fuel the fire.

The best Dutch ovens are cast iron and have flat lids that can be covered with briquettes for extra heat on top. These Dutch ovens have three legs on the bottom to allow you to stack smaller ones on top of larger ones. This is a way to conserve heat and is called "stack cooking." I suggest that you buy a good Dutch oven

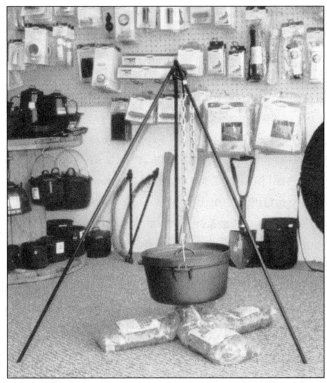

(Photo courtesy of Frontier Survival)

Figure 1.5 Cooking in a Dutch oven is one of the best ways to cook outdoors.

cookbook and learn how to use the equipment. It's an art that takes a little practice.

Outdoor Cooking Methods

Even in nonemergency times, outdoor cooking is extremely popular. Outdoor cooking can also be a great alternative should a crisis prevent us from using our indoor cooking appliances.

Popular outdoor cooking methods including grilling over the fire or roasting meat, vegetables, potatoes, and other foods by wrapping them in aluminum foil. Cook the folded foil packets on top of the coals on a barbecue grill or in a fire pit.

Open Fire

Cooking over an open fire is the oldest and most basic cooking method. Build up the sides around the fire pit with rocks or bricks so you can place an old oven rack or heavy metal screen on top of the fire to hold a pot or frying pan. When the fire dies down and the coals are still hot, you can remove the screen and place a Dutch oven directly on top of the coals to cook your meat, bread, or even a dessert. You'll find it easier to wash your Dutch oven if you soap the bottom before placing it on the fire.

My husband and I have a unique little barbeque pit in our backyard. We use the metal cylinder from an old washing machine to cook on (see figure 1.6). We put wood in the wash tub and start a fire. The tub has many holes for ventilation yet is solid enough that the fire doesn't pop or spit on us. You can also use a metal barrel for burning wood. Just poke holes around the barrel for ventilation. You can then fashion metal screening material into a top for your barrel barbecue.

Barbecue Grills

Backyard barbecue grilling is a great way to prepare meals. Most people already have a barbecue grill on their porch or deck. Just be sure to store extra bottles of propane for your gas grill or bags of charcoal briquettes for regular grills.

Camp Stoves

Many types of camping stoves—as well as ovens that sit on top of them—are available at any retail outdoor store. If you have access to a camper or RV, it may have a nonelectric stove you could use for cooking during a power outage. Again, you will need to store propane or kerosene for fuel.

Figure 1.6 Fire pit made from an old washing machine tub.

Sun or Solar Ovens

Solar ovens, which get their heat from reflective solar power, can be used whenever the sun is out (see figure 1.7). These ovens require no electricity and will bake anything that can be cooked in a regular oven. Solar ovens can be purchased from food storage companies (see Resource Guide).

There are a few sites on the Internet that give the plans for how to make a solar oven out of cardboard and aluminum foil (search the Web for "solar ovens"). Try it for a fun family project in the backyard or the next time you go camping.

Gallon-Can Stove with a Buddy Burner

You can make your own little outdoor camp stove and "buddy burner" from a coffee can or a 1-gallon #10 metal can (common

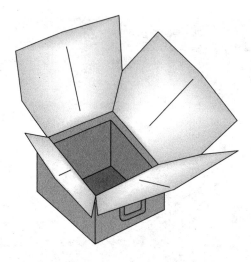

Figure 1.7 A solar oven is heated solely by the sun's rays.

food-storage size). Simply cut a 2-inch by 4-inch opening in the side of the can (see figure 1.8) then use a can opener to make several holes around the top of the can to allow the smoke to escape. Place this stove outdoors on something solid such as concrete, a large rock, or bricks. You can then build a small fire inside the can with sticks, woodchips, or charcoal—or you can use a buddy burner (as described in the next paragraph). You can fry bacon and eggs directly on the top of the can or you can use a small frying pan on the top of the stove.

A buddy burner is a source of fuel that you can make by taking a regular-size (6 1/2-ounce) tuna can and lining it with a strip of corrugated cardboard coiled up inside the can. The strip should be as tall as the can and as long as needed to coil up and fill the entire can. Fill the can with melted paraffin or candle wax. Place a wick or a birthday candle in the center of the buddy burner. When it is lit, place the gallon-size #10 can over the buddy burner and let it heat up. You can use the lid of the tuna can to extinguish the flame

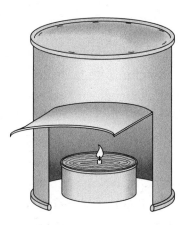

Figure 1.8 Gallon-can stove with a buddy burner.

when you're finished using it. This is a fun project for a family or Scout outing. Kids enjoy making gallon-can stoves.

Outdoor Cooking Equipment and Fuel

❏ Pots and pans

❏ Dutch ovens in several sizes (cast iron)

❏ Frying pan (cast iron)

❏ Kitchen knives

❏ Can opener

❏ Spatula and ladle

❏ Dish towels and rags

❏ Paper plates and cups

❏ Utensils: knifes, forks, spoons

❏ Plastic food storage bags and trash bags

❏ Aluminum foil (heavy duty)

❏ Firewood, briquettes, fuel

❏ Other _____

Alternative Fuel

Fuel is not only difficult to store, but is often hard to come by during crisis situations. Therefore, it's wise to consider alternative fuels, such as wood, coal, charcoal, and others.

Wood and Coal

If you have a wood- or coal-burning stove, you can use it for warmth as well as cook on it. If you are storing wood or coal, be sure to store it where it will stay dry. Wet wood and coal will not burn. Storing these fuels in a coal shed is the best way to keep your wood or coal dry. The following list shows what you will need for cutting wood.

Equipment for Cutting Wood

- ❏ Chain saw
- ❏ Extra sparkplugs
- ❏ Spare chains for chain saw
- ❏ Engine starting fluid (2 cans)
- ❏ Gasoline (8 to 10 gallons)
- ❏ 2-cycle oil (4 quarts)
- ❏ Oil and fuel mixing can
- ❏ Measuring cup
- ❏ Bar chain oil (2 quarts)
- ❏ Axes
- ❏ Wood-splitting mall
- ❏ Bow saw
- ❏ Heavy leather gloves
- ❏ Safety goggles
- ❏ Other _____

Briquettes

Charcoal briquettes are easier to store than wood, and they create quite a hot fire with a relatively small amount of fuel. Because briquettes burn so hot, you can easily burn your food if you use too many of them. For Dutch oven cooking, use nine or ten briquettes on the bottom of the pot and about sixteen briquettes on the top. This would create conditions approximately equal to a 350-degree oven. You can raise or lower the temperature by adding or subtracting about two briquettes for every 25-degree change in temperature. It's better to cook for a longer time period than with a hotter temperature. Take your Dutch oven off the heat with a metal lifter or hot pads and let it cool down for a while before serving the food.

Newspaper Logs

Roll the newspapers from one corner to the other, tucking in the ends as you go and secure the bundle with wire. Next, soak your newspaper logs in water so they shrink up, then dry them out. They will be compact enough to stack easily and will burn very cleanly.

Other Types of Fuel

Other fuels that are available include the following:

- *Propane* can be stored in small tanks and used with a propane camp stove or a propane barbeque grill.
- *Kerosene* or camp fuel can be stored for use in lanterns. Kerosene portable heaters designed with a flat surface on top for cooking are available from sporting-goods stores and food storage companies.
- *Butane* stoves are also available. Butane can be purchased in small canisters and easily stored.
- *Liquid paraffin* lamps, also called liquid candles, are available as well. They last up to 100 hours.

- *Trioxane* is a fuel that comes in bars and can be used to get fires started. You just break off a little piece of the trioxane and quickly start your fire with paper and a small amount of kindling.

Storing Fuels

All fuels should be stored in appropriate storage containers and away from the home in case of a fire. Never store fuel in the same location as you store your food and water. Chemicals in the air can leak into plastic containers and contaminate the contents.

Preparing for Long-Term Emergencies

Once you have prepared your family to deal with short-term emergencies, you can begin equipping yourself for the long term. The chapter ahead will focus on water, our most basic need for survival.

CHAPTER 2

Storing Water for Emergency Use

ATER MAKES up approximately 80 percent of our body weight, and is what we need most for survival. Most of us have experienced the temporary inconvenience of having our water shut off for a few hours. We soon realize how much we depend on being able to turn on a faucet to access water for drinking, cooking, washing, bathing, cleaning, watering plants, and much more. Just recently, my family had an opportunity to use our stored water. A main line up the road from our house broke and the water was shut off for most of the day. We put 2-liter bottles of water in every bathroom for brushing teeth and washing hands and several in the kitchen for cooking and cleaning. People around town were calling to warn each other about this problem. As my friends called, I was happy to report that I had plenty of water stored and that our family would be just fine.

If you were to experience a temporary shortage or a disaster such as a flood and had no water stored, you not only might be unable to access your convenient water supply, but you might have difficulty finding *any* safe water to use.

Water After a Disaster

When a disaster hits, potable water is often the first thing to go. Your personal or community well or the pipes that carry water to your area may be damaged; or the water itself may become contaminated.

In an emergency situation, immediately shut off the water supply to your home. It's a good idea to locate the shut-off valve before you need to use it, and to teach everyone in your family that the water should be shut off right after a disaster. (By the way, the main gas valve must be shut off also!) You can drain the pipes and collect the water that is left in your water lines, which will not yet be contaminated. Just turn on the faucet that is located in the highest room of the house to let air into the lines, then draw the water from the lowest faucet of the house.

Storing Emergency Water

I can't emphasize enough the importance of storing clean water for emergencies. If you use contaminated water for drinking or cooking, it can cause symptoms such as stomachaches, nausea, vomiting, diarrhea, or fever. It can also lead to life-threatening illnesses such as hepatitis, cholera, amebic dysentery, viral infections, and typhoid fever. It's best to have clean water available so you don't have to risk such consequences. If you haven't stored water, be sure you take precautions and disinfect your water before you use it (see "Methods of Sanitizing Water for Storage" later in this chapter).

How Much Water to Store

Each person in your family will need a 72-hour emergency supply of water. To calculate how much you should store, figure approximately one gallon per person per day for drinking, plus an additional gallon per day for washing, cooking, sponge bathing, laundry, dishes, and so on (a total of two gallons per day for each person). For a 72-hour supply, you'll need to store six gallons per person.

I recommend a three-month supply of water if possible. This is approximately 180 gallons per person (90 gallons for drinking and 90 gallons for extra cooking and washing). Children, nursing mothers, and sick people may require more so store a little extra for them. There are several ways to store this much water. First, it's helpful to understand what water you can safely store, and how you can purify it if necessary.

What Water to Use

Just about any fresh water can be safely stored and used. Sources for obtaining water include the following:

Bottled Water
Bulk bottled water can be purchased through companies such as Culligan, Mt. Olympus, Coca-Cola, or PepsiCo. The bottles come in boxes and can be stacked. You can purchase larger quantities at discount prices. Although today's grocery stores carry bottled water in an array of sizes and types, it is generally far too expensive to store in any quantity—even if used exclusively for drinking.

Tap Water
Tap water that comes from a municipal water system contains enough chlorine to be safe for long-term water storage. Just fill your clean containers with tap water and store them away from sunlight.

Supplemental Sources of Water

If you don't yet have a stash of emergency water, or prefer to reserve it as long as possible, you can take advantage of other available sources of water. The water in your hot water heater, for example, is available to use. Be sure to shut off the incoming water or intake valve to avoid contaminated water mixing with the safe water. To take water out of the tank, open the drain valve. You can attach a hose to this valve and drain your hot water tank into containers.

The water in the tank of the toilet (not the bowl!) can be scooped out and used if needed.

Liquids for drinking can be obtained from canned fruits, juices, vegetables, and soft drinks, or anything that has been water-packed in the canning process.

You can also use melted snow or rain water if you have a collection barrel. You can use any large, clean container for collecting water. Be sure to disinfect the water before drinking it. Boiling it vigorously for five minutes will kill all bacteria.

Swimming pools or spas contain water that can be used, if boiled first, for washing but should *not* be used for drinking. Lakes, streams, ponds, rivers, and even ditches contain water that you can drink if it is clarified and treated with one of the following sanitizing methods.

Methods of Sanitizing Water for Storage

If your water supply is cut off or contaminated, an emergency supply of water stored at home is a good way to insure that you have a safe water supply. If you stored it properly, then you can rely upon it. If you must use water that is unsafe, or you aren't sure whether it is entirely safe, be sure to purify it first. The following water treatment methods reduce the risk of bacterial growth that can make people get sick when they drink it or suffer from skin conditions if they wash themselves or their clothes with it.

Home Purification Devices

Do not rely on water filters or home purifiers to substitute for properly stored water. If you use a water filter or home purifier, you must still purify the water by boiling or using a chemical. Reverse osmosis devices and home distillers cannot be relied upon to remove grossly contaminated water, but they can remove chlorine or iodine after the water has been safely disinfected by another method. Using a water purifier will greatly improve the taste of disinfected water.

Boiling Method

The safest method of purifying water is to boil it vigorously for five minutes. To improve the taste of the water after it has been boiled, pour the water from one container to another to aerate it. Do not use cloudy water if you have a choice between clear or cloudy. Cloudy water may be caused by bacterial growth, therefore must be strained through a cloth to remove the particles then boiled or treated with chemicals before it is consumed.

Stabilized Oxygen Method

According to many studies, stabilized oxygen products (such as ION) are very effective for water purification. These products will kill giardia and the bacteria that cause cholera within a few minutes. Although their high levels of oxygen are lethal to anaerobic bacteria and other organisms, these products are safe for humans and don't have any of the harmful side effects that are associated with chlorine or iodine. (See Resource Guide for sources.)

It only takes a few drops to purify a glass of water and about 20 drops to purify 1 gallon. I suggest you use this method for drinking water only. Water that will be boiled for dishes or laundry does not need to be purified with stabilized oxygen.

Chemical Sterilization Using Bleach

You can purify water by adding any household bleach that is not too old. When you buy bleach, mark your purchase date on the label. Use it within a year, as it loses effectiveness over time. The most common bleach solutions contain 5.25 percent sodium hypochlorite. Add the appropriate amount of bleach to water (see table 1) and mix thoroughly by stirring or shaking it. Then let it stand for 30 minutes so the bleach can do its job. Do not use lemon-scented or perfumed bleach.

Tincture of Iodine

You can use ordinary 2 percent tincture of iodine, which you may have in your medicine cabinet to purify small quantities of water.

TABLE 1. Water-Bleach Ratio for Purification

Amount of Water to Purify	Amount of Bleach to Add to Clear Water	Amount of Bleach to Add to Cloudy Water
1 quart	2 drops	4 drops
1 gallon	8 drops	16 drops
5 gallons	1/2 teaspoon	1 teaspoon

Add three drops of tincture of iodine to each quart of clear water or six drops to each quart of cloudy water. Stir well and let it stand for thirty minutes. This process will kill all bacteria, but the water will be a brownish-red color and will have a slight taste of iodine. Pregnant women and people with thyroid problems should not use this method.

Water Purification Tablets

Water purification tablets release chlorine or iodine to purify the water. Because they are often used by backpackers and hikers, you can purchase them at most sporting goods stores or drugstores. These tablets have a shelf life of five years unopened.

Halazone Tablets

Halazone tablets for water disinfection are commonly carried by emergency room technicians or paramedics for emergency sterilization. They can be purchased in drugstores. The shelf life of these tablets is only two years, so check the label to see how long they have been on the drugstore shelf before you purchase them. Keep these tablets tightly sealed. If the tablets turn yellow or smell bad, do not use them. Again, allow the water to stand at least thirty minutes after you've added the halazone before drinking it. This gives the chemicals time to work.

How to Store Water

To properly store water after you have either verified its purity or sanitized it yourself, you must choose suitable containers and select appropriate locations at your home. Water is best stored in a dark room or in heavy cardboard boxes to keep the light out. Store

Radioactive Contamination

There is no safe method for treating water that contains nuclear radioactive fallout. It's much better to use stored water that you know is safe.

your water supply in several locations so you can get to it easily. I like to store most of my water in smaller containers because they are much easier to carry around.

Containers to Use

You can use any of the many types of containers available for water storage. My favorite way to store water is in heavy plastic containers, which are relatively lightweight yet durable.

Make sure all containers used for water storage are food grade and have never previously held chemicals or poisons. All containers need to be cleaned thoroughly because whatever was in the container will leach into the water and make it taste bad.

Heavy Plastic

Rather than buy new containers, save and reuse heavy-gauge plastic beverage containers. Two-liter soda bottles work best for storing water. Gatorade, apple juice, or cranberry juice bottles are great also. Rinse them out well before you fill them with water. I save all of the heavy plastic jugs that come into my house, fill them with water to about one inch from the top to allow for expansion in case the water freezes, then seal them with tight-fitting lids and store them in my basement and garage. Unlike foods, purified water can be safely stored where temperatures fluctuate from hot to freezing.

Bleach Bottles

Plastic bleach bottles can be used for water storage simply by filling the bottle with water and sealing it with a tight-fitting lid. I recommend that you do not drink the water stored in bleach bottles, but use it for cleaning or washing hands. Label it clearly with a black marker. Keep these containers away from children so they don't accidentally confuse the real bleach with water and drink it.

Polyethylene Barrels

Commercial water storage barrels are available in several sizes. To store a large amount of water, you can obtain 55-gallon drums made of plastic polyethylene from most food storage or emergency supply companies (see figure 2.1). If you fill a 55-gallon drum with water, it will become so heavy that it cannot be moved. You will therefore need a permanent location as well as a pump or spigot so you can get the water into smaller containers.

You can also find smaller drums that hold 5 to 6 gallons of water. When filled, even these weigh more than 40 pounds so they would also require a pump for convenient use. These smaller drums are nice, though, because they can be moved much more easily than the 55-gallon drums.

Glass Containers

Drinking water can be stored in quart-sized jars sealed by the water-bath canning method. Fill the jars with water, leaving a head space of about 1 inch, then tighten the lid and ring onto the jar. Boil the jars in a water bath or use a steam canner. Pint jars require 20 minutes' boiling time, quart jars require 25 minutes, and

(Photo courtesy of Maple Leaf Foods)

Figure 2.1 Water storage barrels

half-gallon jars require 30 minutes. Store the jars with cardboard between them so they don't break.

Milk Jugs

Milk jugs may seem appropriate, but they are not good containers in which to store water. After about six months these containers start to biodegrade, collapse, and leak. You are likely to have a big mess—as well as no water available in a time of emergency.

Shelf Life of Water

As water sits over time, disease organisms tend to die. So the longer water is stored properly—using one of the methods described—the safer it becomes from the growth of bacteria.

Checking Your Water Supply

Although you need not rotate your water as you would stored food, you should check it occasionally for cloudiness and leakage. If the water looks or tastes bad, then change it. If the water tastes flat, you can pour it back and forth between containers to aerate it or whip it to introduce more oxygen into the water.

Water is the most important item to include in your storage program. While you can survive without food for at least 72 hours, you cannot live long without water. Fortunately, water can withstand temperature extremes, be safely stored in many types of recycled containers, and does not require regular rotation. It also costs little to nothing to replace in nonemergency situations. Storing food, however, is a much greater challenge than storing water; therefore food storage will be the focus of the chapters ahead.

CHAPTER 3

The Economics
of Long-Term
Emergency Storage

Y OU MIGHT be thinking that long-term emergency storage sounds like a good idea, but are wondering whether it's worth the high cost. After all, you might ask yourself, how likely is a real crisis? Besides, you may find it difficult enough just to pay your current bills, let alone keep emergency cash on hand. You may find that buying groceries for the week stretches your budget, and wonder how anyone could store enough for months—or for an entire year. This chapter will tell you what emergency storage is and what it is not, detail the economic advantages of preparing for the future, and explain how you can not only pay off your debts and finance your emergency store, but progress toward an even more provident future.

Planning for Long-Term Emergencies

How one thinks about and plans for emergency storage has great impact not only on whether it is successful, but whether it is affordable and cost-effective. When people think of emergency storage, many envision something very different from what I recommend in this book. Mistaken attitudes often result in wasted food, wasted money, wasted time, as well as a false sense of security.

Mistaken Attitudes Regarding Emergency Storage

Some people buy as much food as they can for the money they have and simply stick it away for an emergency. They may spend all their funds purchasing a large amount of wheat, beans, rice, dry milk, dried fruits, dried vegetables, and honey; then they think, "I'm prepared," and hope they never have to eat it. Ten years later they throw it all out.

Others think, "I'll just use the chart in the food storage book I bought and that should be good enough." The problem with this plan is that no food storage chart—however nutritious and practical it may be—is personalized for your family. Therefore, if you buy exactly what a chart says, you may waste much of your money. Your family might not like the food, and may even refuse to eat it. And there's always a chance that someone will experience allergic reactions to a certain food and find it impossible to eat.

In addition, if you are not accustomed to cooking with the listed foods, it's likely that you simply will not use it. As a consequence, the food you store will not be rotated but will sit on the shelf until it expires. If, for example, you are not accustomed to using whole wheat in your baking or haven't developed the skills of bread making and cooking from scratch, you're unlikely to miraculously change when you are faced with a crisis. Change is much more difficult under stress.

Another problem is that people store their emergency food in out-of-the-way places such as attics, garages, or basements. Because it's not convenient for them to get to the food, they don't use it. Storing food in its original packages or in unacceptable storage containers is also a common problem, as is storing the food in temperatures that are either too high or fluctuate a great deal. Exposure to hot summers and cold winters, for example, will deteriorate food and destroy its nutritive value faster than any other conditions. (See chapter 4 for more on storage specifics.)

Another typical problem is that people buy bulk food that may be old or have lower nutritional value. Foods that are on sale may be so because they are near or even past their shelf life. What may seem a good deal is no bargain if the food is already dated.

Hopefully you won't make any of these common mistakes when implementing your food storage program. Nor will you make the mistake of simply not bothering to prepare until you see a crisis situation coming, then panic and start buying up as much food as you can get. Panic purchasing could cost you many times more than what you would have spent had you planned ahead. Reading this book will help you avoid these and other typical problems people encounter when storing foods.

A Practical Plan for Long-Term Emergency Storage

Now that you've read the mistaken attitudes and learned what emergency storage should not be, it's time to clarify what it should be. First, thinking of long-term emergency storage as a cost-effective investment rather than an excessive expense will help provide you with motivation to begin storing food—as well as help you establish a successful and practical storage program.

A practical plan is simply this: Use what you store, and store what you use. In other words, you won't be spending money on food and supplies that will be tucked away and never used (when you're fortunate enough to avoid any crisis that requires you to use your emergency supplies!). Instead, this plan involves simply storing extra amounts of items your family already consumes, using the oldest items before they expire, and rotating the new items into storage. You can gradually increase your family's stockpile, a little at a time, until you have enough to see you through a week-long crisis, then enough for a month, then a three-month supply, then a six-month supply, until you reach your ultimate goal.

Your "home grocery store" will be to you and your family what the ark was to Noah and his family. It will contain all the necessary food, water, bedding, clothing, fuel, cooking equipment, and medical supplies to sustain life for a minimum of three months to one year.

If you don't properly plan your emergency storage, then it will be a haphazard process. Several families from our local church discovered the importance of careful planning when they were challenged to live on their food storage for as long as possible without going to the grocery store for anything. They found doing so very difficult because they were missing essential ingredients such as spices, oil, sugar, eggs, milk, cheese, juices, meat, fruits, vegetables, and condiments. If you don't carefully plan, you will lack necessary ingredients, or your meals may be bland and perhaps not even nutritious.

A food storage program based on planned menus can eliminate the panic you may feel when you know you should store food but don't know where to begin. Also, careful planning will enable you to avoid impulse or panic buying. A practical food storage plan will be nutritious, comprehensive, and tailored to your family.

Store Nutritious Foods

Most people store the cheaper bulk foods such as rice, wheat, beans, powdered milk, and honey, but you can't make nutritious meals out of these ingredients alone. Without other essential ingredients, the food you prepare will lack the necessary nutrients and taste bland.

People on diets that have little variety often develop what is called *appetite fatigue,* which can be a very serious condition. Symptoms include stomach problems, dehydration, diarrhea, vomiting, and a total lack of interest in food. Children and elderly people are especially vulnerable to appetite fatigue. If they don't like the food they're given, they simply won't eat it. If you are suddenly forced into eating a diet to which you are not accustomed—wheat, beans, and dehydrated foods, for example—you may get very sick. One thing you don't need during a crisis is sickness caused by a drastic change in your diet. During a crisis is not a good time to change your family's diet.

Store the Foods Your Family Eats

There is nothing wrong with storing wheat, rice, beans, and dehydrated food—if that is what you are accustomed to, like, and can tolerate. If your family eats these foods then by all means include them in your food storage plan. If your family doesn't eat it now, however, they probably won't eat it during a crisis.

You can store a variety of grains (not just wheat), flour, oatmeal, rice, noodles, evaporated milk, beans, peas, lentils, canned meats, tuna, canned salmon, soup of all kinds, tomatoes, sauces of all kinds, all baking items, shortening, oil, peanut butter, jams, syrups, salad dressings, mayonnaise, gelatin, cocoa, bottled fruits and vegetables, and many other dehydrated products. In other words, store whatever you would need to maintain your family's current diet as much as possible.

Store Enough to Meet Your Family's Needs

It is necessary to plan carefully to be sure you have enough of each item you use. Haphazard buying and storing may leave you with plenty of starches, but no protein foods—or plenty of beans, but no spices to make them palatable. A sample formula for calculating how much food to store is to keep track of what you eat for a one-week period of time—not just the main ingredients, but *all* ingredients. (Surprisingly, most families repeat meals every few days, so this isn't as hard as you might expect.) Then multiply the basic ingredients by twelve to calculate a three-month supply, by twenty-six for a six-month supply, and by fifty-two to calculate a one-year supply. You can calculate separate menus for summer and winter, taking into consideration gardening and seasonal foods that are available. (See chapter 7 for gardening ideas.)

Economic Advantage of Long-Term Storage

Not only will you be providing an invaluable form of insurance for your family—one that will assure that they will be fed, clothed, and sheltered during times of crisis—emergency storage will also enable you to benefit economically. For example, you'll be able to better avoid waste and to buy more efficiently for the long term than when buying on impulse or demand.

Avoid Waste

Improper planning causes waste. Most of us have experienced buying too many fresh vegetables or too much fruit, then having to throw out what doesn't get eaten. Storing food requires that we plan ahead and preserve items for future use. As long as we "store what we eat" by selecting only what we will actually use, carefully store the food so that it remains usable, and "eat what we store" before it expires, we can avoid waste.

I know many people who have purchased items that their family didn't like or wouldn't eat. Then five to ten years later, they got rid of it at a yard sale or at the dump. I also know people who purchased food in bulk, and the mice and insects got into it because it was never properly sealed in airtight containers. I've seen bags of wheat thrown out to the pigs. I've seen opened bags of muffin or pancake mix get infested with weevils and other bugs and have to be thrown out. I've seen little black beetles get into sugar. I've seen sugar go hard like cement because moisture got into bags that were stored in a garage.

Without proper buckets and containers, food is subject to many factors that cause deterioration. So you can fully realize the economic advantages of avoiding waste, follow the recommendations given in chapter 4 on how to properly store food. Also read the information in chapter 6 on canning and bottling fruits and vegetables so you can take full advantage of your own garden or the abundance of in-season produce.

Prepare for Tomorrow Without Shorting Yourself Today

Going into debt for your food storage is *not* recommended.

Simply build your stockpile slowly, just as you would a savings account, a little each month. Over a one-year period of time, for example, you can start with a short-term supply, then build your stockpile to sustain you for three months, then six months, then nine months, continuing until you have collected a full year's supply. It's important that you have a plan that includes a list of the items and amounts of each item you will need. If you find a good buy on something, you can check your list and, if you need it, buy it. Having a plan rather than buying on impulse can save you thousands of dollars.

Hint: Every time you go to the grocery store, get two of each item that you normally buy, such as ketchup, barbecue sauce,

Save Money

Food in the pantry is better than money in the bank.

It's certainly okay to have money in the bank, but it may not be accessible or usable when you need it. During hard times in the past, banks have been shut down or accounts frozen. If this were to happen, it would probably be too late to implement a food storage program for your family. For those reasons, it's important that you first attend to your food storage needs.

Food storage also enables families to purchase much more efficiently. By buying for several months or a year at a time, you can buy in bulk and take advantage of seasonal sales. You can purchase cases of items when they come on sale, for example. Our hometown grocery store has case lot sales about four times a year. I buy wet-pack corn and beans in the fall when they are sold at three cans for $1.00. When tuna (an excellent source of protein!) goes on sale, I buy five or six cases.

pickles, olives, cream soups, mayonnaise, salad dressing, spaghetti sauces, and mixes. Put one away and use the other—and always replace each item as you use it up so you can maintain your stockpile. It's a good idea to keep adding a greater variety of items to your home grocery store so your diet won't be bland.

By building your stockpile gradually, you should be able to avoid spending a large amount of cash up front. If you plan carefully, you will be able to stash some cash as well as stock your cupboards.

Stash Some Cash for Emergencies

In addition to financing the purchase of your emergency store, you will need at least a three-month stash of money to pay for all expenses in case you lose your job, get hurt, or experience any other emergency that prevents you from providing for your family. If you face an unexpected setback—such as job loss, illness, or accident—and have no paycheck coming in or savings that you could access, you'll either have to borrow cash to cover your bills and necessary expenses, or risk serious consequences. If you are barely making ends meet now, you'll need to start from the beginning, by preparing a realistic budget.

Prepare a Budget

Complete table 2 so you can calculate how much money you need to sustain your family during an emergency.

Note: Do not put your emergency fund money in the bank. If times are tough and the economy fails, you won't have ready access to it. Instead, put your cash stash away in a fireproof safe so you'll always have quick cash necessary to live on. Once you have saved enough cash to see your family through at least three months, make a promise to yourself that you will not use this stash for anything but what it was intended for.

Be sure that you have the "correct change." Small bills and coins are much easier to use, and businesses may not take large bills during a crisis situation. For your emergency stash, approximately one-third should be coins, one-third should be small bills (under $20), and one-third should be $20 and $50 bills. You also can put some silver and gold coins away in case regular currency loses its value.

TABLE 2. Monthly Expenses

Expense	Amount
House payment	
Utilities	
Telephone	
Food	
Clothing	
Car payments	
Gasoline	
Car insurance	
Health insurance	
Medical and dental expenses	
Education expenses	
Fixed debts	
Credit card payments	
Other	
Other	
Total Needed Per Month	
Total Needed for Three Months	
Total Needed for Six Months	

Get Out and Stay Out of Debt

You may be among the many people who find it difficult to pay the bills or get through a single month, let alone gather the emergency cash to see themselves through three months! It is wise, therefore, to get out of debt and stay out by paying as you go, thus living within your income. This one principle alone has brought my husband and me the greatest peace of mind.

If you are currently living beyond your means and owe money that you don't have, prepare a plan to get out of debt. One way is to increase your income. For example, you might take an extra job or find creative ways to earn extra cash. What products or services can you sell for profit? What unneeded items could you sell for additional money? You'll be amazed how quickly you can come up with ideas for gathering extra money when you focus on it.

Another way is to decrease your spending. If your get-out-of-debt plan is going to work, it's very important for you to cut up your credit cards and cancel them. Otherwise, it's much too easy to use a card to spend money you don't have. If you don't have the money for what you want, then you simply don't buy it. If it's important enough, you can save up for it.

Although you can certainly improve your financial situation by simply increasing your income, decreasing your spending, or doing some of each, these methods work best when you have carefully assessed your budget and adopted a family financial plan.

CHAPTER 4

The Logistics of Long-Term Emergency Storage

NCE YOU'VE completed your survival plan and have prepared your family to handle short-term emergencies, you'll want to begin stocking your store for longer-term survival. You can set your own goals to fit the amount of space you have available for storage, the amount of money you can afford to spend, and the amount of time you have to obtain the items for storage. You can, for example, begin by storing enough to see you through a month-long emergency, then expand your storage to cover longer time periods (such as three months, then six months) until you reach your ultimate goal, perhaps the full year's supply that I recommend.

In this chapter you'll learn about the various options for locating your home storage. You'll also read about factors that decrease shelf life of stored food and how you can prolong shelf life by using appropriate storage containers, properly removing the oxygen from the containers, and sealing them for long-term storage.

Where to Locate Your Home Grocery Store and Pharmacy

Before storing food and supplies, you'll need to select a place that will best meet the criteria for appropriate conditions, relative convenience, and sufficient space. Look around your home and property. Find a room that you can dedicate as your home grocery store, or in which you can make space for your store.

Finding the Best Conditions for Storage

Store your food in a cool, dry place away from sunlight that stays a constant temperature, between 40 and 60 degrees F. This is important because hot or cold fluctuations in temperatures can destroy the nutritive value of the food and shorten its shelf life.

Find the coolest place in your house. This will usually be in your basement (if you have one), but preferably away from a furnace room or other heat source. Freezer, refrigerators, furnaces, and water heaters should not be located in this room because they all give off heat, increasing the room temperature.

Other good locations are root cellars, insulated and heated garages (where the temperature stays constant between 40 and 60 degrees F), spare bedrooms, unfinished rooms, crawl spaces, closets, under stairways, or under beds. North walls are cooler because they are away from sun exposure.

The room you choose should stay dry at all times. If your clothes dryer is located in this room, be sure it is properly ventilated to prevent moisture from gathering on the food.

Choosing Your Most Convenient Space

Remember: The closer you can locate your food storage area to your kitchen, the easier you will find it to rotate the food. The following are some locations you might consider for your home store.

The Basement

If you are lucky enough to have a basement, you will find that the temperature is usually cooler, ideal for storing food (see figure 4.1). Keep all food away from dryer vents or furnaces, which give off moisture that can rust your cans.

Under the Stairways

There is usually a lot of wasted space under a stairway since the sloped ceiling makes it inappropriate for a living area. Shelves can be built that will hold canned goods, large buckets, as well as camping equipment, 72-hour kits, medical supplies, and so on. *Hint:* Try installing hooks from the ceiling to hold your 72-hour backpacks.

Figure 4.1 I use stackable plastic cheese crates (with one side cut out) to keep my food storage organized.

Closets

A pantry can be made out of a closet (see figure 4.2). You'll be amazed at how much a closet will hold when the shelving is installed properly. Be sure to measure all your boxes or cans so you can make the shelving just the right size to hold the food, without

Figure 4.2 You can easily make a closet into a pantry.

leaving any more wasted space than necessary. I like to build the first shelf high enough off the floor (or ground) so several six-gallon buckets can be stored underneath. I keep all my bulk food such as rice, beans, sugar, flour, wheat, pasta, and dried potatoes in buckets so I can easily slide them out, take what I need, and use it.

The Garage

If the temperature in your garage fluctuates between freezing in the winter and hot in the summer, then your garage isn't the best place for food. Food retains its nutritive value approximately 50 percent longer when it stays at a relatively constant temperature than when stored in extremely uneven temperatures.

However, a garage is a great place for all the short-term emergency equipment and kits, as well as nonfood items such as extra toilet paper and paper towels. If your garage temperature goes below 32 degrees F in the winter, you can store grain and beans there because the freezing temperatures will kill bugs.

The Attic

Do not store food in your attic if it heats up in the summer (most attics do). The food will spoil quickly in hot temperatures. If your attic is vented and insulated and stays a fairly constant temperature, it will be just fine. Remember, however, that the farther away from the kitchen the food is stored, the harder it will be for you to get to and rotate it. If your attic is fairly close to your kitchen and easily accessible by stairs or a pull-down ladder, it may work just fine for you.

The Utility Room

If large enough, your utility room may well double as a room for food storage. Shelves can be built above the washer and dryer to store extra laundry soap, bleach, and other cleaners. I had two feet of wasted space along one wall in my utility room, so I had shelves built along the entire wall. The top shelf holds all my canning and sprouting equipment, wheat grinder, juicer, and large roasting pans, along with extra blankets, pillows, sleeping bags, and more.

Figure 4.3 My utility room provides convenient food storage space.

The side shelves were built to hold all my spices, which I buy in bulk and store in plastic containers, as well as my gallon-size containers of food. The center has two rolling self-feeding units that hold twenty cases of canned goods. They can be pulled in and out to stock the shelves from the back. I love my utility room now; it is very organized and holds a lot of food and food-preparation equipment (see figure 4.3). In addition, it's close to my kitchen, which makes it convenient for me to rotate and use foods stored there.

The Kitchen

My kitchen cupboards are full of clear plastic containers, such as those made by Rubbermaid or Tupperware. I put food that I use often in these containers. The contents of a gallon-size (#10) can will fit just right into these plastic containers and the containers fit nicely on our kitchen shelves. Although they're clear and we generally can see what's in them at a glance, I still label the fronts so I know exactly what's in each container and date it so I know precisely when it was opened. It is best to use darker containers, which block more light than clear or neutral-colored containers. You can purchase dark plastic containers for bulk food items and spices through some of the food storage supply companies listed in the Resource Guide.

Ideas for Tight Quarters and Apartment Dwellers

If you live in a small house where space is very limited, that doesn't mean you can't prepare for at least short-term emergencies by storing extra food and supplies. Because you will probably want to disguise your stockpile the best you can, I've included some suggestions that will make your stash practically invisible—and sometimes even practical or decorative! You can use your own imagination to come up with clever disguises. Here are a few ideas for storing food when extra space is scarce.

Under the Bed

Because the space under most beds is usually empty, it can be a good place to store cases of food, which hold six #10-size cans. Case goods from the grocery store, such as green beans and corn, fit nicely under beds also.

You can either just slide the cases under the bed frame or put the mattress right on top of the boxes (see figure 4.4). Because cases of cans stack nicely, you could create a large stockpile of canned goods under a single mattress. To disguise, simply cover the boxes with a dust ruffle. Be sure to label each box with what is in it, and keep a master list of what you have and where it is stored. Only store the items that you won't be using in the near future, as the more out of the way the storage space is, the harder it will be to get to.

In Bookcases

You can also use #10 cans to make bookshelves or shelves to store more cans of food. Put a board across four cans (two at each end) and stack more cans on top of the boards (see figure 4.5). (If the board is long enough to sag under the weight of additional cans, add

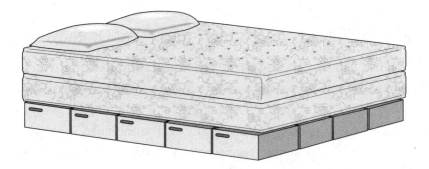

Figure 4.4 Under the bed can be a good place to store cases of food.

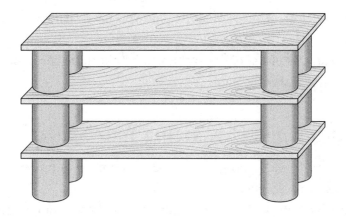

Figure 4.5 Shelves provide lots of storage space.

another #10 can or two in the middle for additional support.) Keep doing this until you feel your shelf is tall enough yet still stable.

As End Tables and Coffee Tables
A five- or six-gallon bucket can become an attractive end table (see figure 4.6). Place a round piece of wood on top of the can, cover it

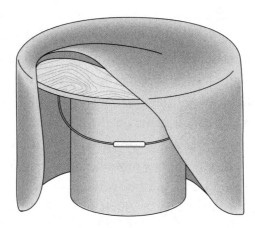

Figure 4.6 A bucket containing stored food can double as an end table.

with a tablecloth or piece of fabric, and you have created a piece of furniture!

You can also store food inside a trunk or antique chest that you can then use as a coffee table.

Preparing and Organizing Your Space

Once you've found appropriate space, you'll need to properly prepare it for food storage.

Seal all cracks and crevices where mice or insects might get in. Keep mouse D-Con hidden in the room (making sure the poison is not accessible to pets or children). Mice will ruin the food in any unsealed buckets or cardboard containers. I learned from experience after personally having to throw away food, especially wrapped items such as MREs (meals ready to eat), because mice got into it. The mice also ate right through the metal foil of yeast packages, which caused my yeast to explode. I now keep all such items in buckets with properly sealed lids.

Moth infestation is another common problem. The little worm larvae also eat right through metal foil pouches. Heavy plastic containers, jars, or metal cans with tight-fitting lids will keep both mice and insects out. Another suggestion is to stick a bay leaf in with grains, flour, beans, legumes, and other items to keep them from getting bug-infested. Weevils do not like the smell of bay leaves and will stay away from anything containing them.

Do not leave any food items on the shelves for any length of time that have not been sealed properly. Also, if any food spills, clean it up immediately. If your room becomes bug-infested, clean out all infested food items and throw them away. Remove all food and equipment, and then spray all shelves (including cracks and crevices) with an insecticide such as Malathion or Diazinon. Let the chemical sit for ten minutes to eradicate any pests, larvae, or eggs, and then clean the shelves. Do not store these chemicals in the same room as the food.

Keeping Stored Supplies off the Ground

If your storage room has dirt floors or cement, use wooden pallets or bricks with wood across them to elevate the food up off the floor. The containers should never come in contact with the ground. Moisture from the ground will rust the cans and can get into the buckets. Also, the air must be able to circulate around the food to keep it dry. Keep the powdered milk and other dairy products, dried eggs, and oils closer to the floor level so they stay cooler.

Providing Shelving

If you can find a place in your home to put shelves, you can conveniently store a large amount of food and supplies in relatively little space. An easy and relatively inexpensive way to add shelving is to purchase metal shelves that you assemble yourself. Such shelves come in various sizes so you can put them in any location in your home or garage. Closets usually include some wasted space in which you can put shelves, and work well for food storage.

Shelves should be designed so that a simple rotation system can effectively allow the oldest food to be used first and the newest food to be rotated within the shelf-life period. Shelving that's against the wall should not be so deep that rotation becomes a chore. If possible, consider shelves that can be rolled away from the wall or can be accessed from both sides so you can retrieve goods for use from the "front" side and stock at the "back" side. An ideal alternative is to build and install self-feeding shelves (see figure 4.7). These shelves have a 2-inch drop from back to front that allows cans to roll forward. You stock them from the back, the

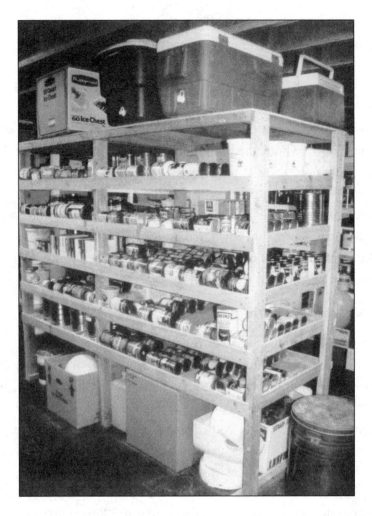

Figure 4.7 Self-feeding shelves help ensure proper rotation of your stored foods.

cans roll down, and you use the cans from the front, ensuring proper rotation of your stored foods.

You can custom design your home grocery store and pharmacy to exactly what your family needs. Figures 4.8 and 4.9 are examples of some well-planned and organized shelving that may give you some ideas that would work well for you.

Figure 4.8 Corner shelving unit.

Avoiding Deterioration of Stored Foods

Stored food requires much more careful handling than stored water. Not only will it fare far better when temperatures remain relatively constant and cool, but it is susceptible to deterioration as well as rodent and insect infestation if not properly stored.

As mentioned earlier, stockpiling food can enable you to save money and avoid waste—but only if you are able to consume it. That's why understanding what can cause food to become inedible and knowing how you can prevent it from happening is so important. This information will enable you to select proper containers that will ensure that your food stays edible as long as possible.

Figure 4.9 These shelves were built to accommodate water barrels and bags of wheat underneath.

Shelf Life

Even when you do everything to ensure that your food is protected from the elements and insects, food will eventually lose its freshness if left on the shelf too long. Therefore, it's important that you first understand the concept of "shelf life." Foods are considered to have a "life" time during which they remain suitable for use, and after which they are not recommended for human consumption.

When food is stored too long, two things happen: The nutritional value breaks down, and the color, flavor, texture, and smell change to the point that most people will not want to eat it.

Do not allow food that you store to surpass its shelf life so you must throw it away. Rotate your food and use it within the estimated period of time determined by research done on each product. For example, dehydrated dairy products and eggs will store approximately five years; dehydrated fruits and vegetables will store seven years; and grains, beans, and legumes will store ten years or more. Wheat can store up to twenty years or longer. Commercially canned foods should be rotated within two years. However, these rules apply *only* when foods have been properly canned and sealed with low oxygen content, and are stored at the ideal temperature. Table 3 provides a good rule of thumb for the shelf life of canned and dehydrated foods.

TABLE 3. Shelf Life of Commonly Stored Foods

Food	Approximate Shelf Life
Dried foods (opened)	1 year
All canned goods	2 years
All dried dairy products	5 years
All dried fruits and vegetables	7 years
All beans and other legumes	7 years
All grains	10 years
Wheat	10 to 20 years

Causes of Deterioration and Spoilage

In addition to its limited shelf life, food is susceptible to deterioration and spoilage that results from a variety of natural causes. The following are a few of the most common problems that result in food expiring before its estimated shelf life.

Oxygen

Oxygen will rob food of its nutritive value. All living food contains enzymes that, when exposed to oxygen, start to break down the food by a process known as oxidation. Nutritive value is lost little by little as food breaks down. That is why it is important to remove the oxygen from the containers before you seal them. It's also good to store grains as whole rather than cracked grain. Once the kernel is ground, it starts to lose its nutritive value and the rancidity process begins.

Bacteria

Bacteria, yeast, and molds are controlled by several methods: processing, canning, dehydrating, drying, or freezing. Bacteria is the most common cause of spoilage, so it is important to make sure all food is properly processed, by whichever method you choose. Once containers of processed beans, meat, vegetables, and other foods are opened and cooked, you must quickly use up the food to prevent spoilage. For example, wet-packed beans that have retained their food value in a vacuum-sealed can for two years will spoil within a matter of days once the can has been opened. Always refrigerate wet-packed foods (those packed in water, juice, or other liquid) once they have been opened.

Insects

Insects grow in food because the eggs or larvae are either already in the product before it is packaged or are able to get inside improperly sealed packages.

The most common insects found in foods are ants, roaches, earwigs, moths, silver fish, beetles, and weevils. They not only get into the food, but they eat it, deposit their waste products in it, and lay eggs in it. The eggs then hatch and result in infestation.

Light

As you collect containers for your bulk food, try to get ones that are dark and cannot be permeated by light. The two containers that most commonly allow light inside are glass jars (or bottles) and plastic buckets. If you use glass or light-colored plastic containers, you should store them in heavy cardboard boxes or in a dark room.

Temperature

A cool dark place is a must for food storage. The temperature of the room should stay relatively constant throughout the year. The ideal temperature is between 40 and 60 degrees F, which is the range of most basements. If the temperature is higher than 60 degrees, it will slightly cut down the shelf life of your stored food. If you store your food in a garage, shed, or attic where the temperature fluctuates from very hot to very cold, you could be cutting down the shelf life of your food to half the time listed on the shelf-life chart.

Humidity and Moisture

Humidity and moisture promote the deterioration of most foods, which is the principle behind dehydrating foods. Because the moisture level of dehydrated foods should remain under 10 percent, they store best when the moisture is removed from the air so they won't prematurely rehydrate and spoil. Dehydrated food will be hard, but should not be leathery.

Be sure to keep all containers up off the floor and away from anything that tends to raise the humidity level, such as dryer vents, water heaters, or anything that could flood (such as a clothes washer, dishwasher, sink, or shower) and damage the food.

Prevention of Deterioration and Spoilage

Besides avoiding the elements that result in food deterioration, you can take additional steps that will further retard spoilage. You can use any of several methods, depending on what food you are storing, what containers you are using, and what food storage problems you are most likely to face.

Oxygen Absorber Packets

Oxygen absorber packets look like tea bags or sugar packets. This relatively new procedure for retarding spoilage is proving to be one of the best methods. These packets absorb the oxygen from the container and trap it in the iron powder and salt mixture. This is the safest way to remove oxygen. After inserting the oxygen packet into your container, seal the container properly.

Note: Oxygen absorber packets must be used up within fifteen minutes of being opened and exposed to the air. If you have several packets left after opening a bag of them, put them in a glass jar with a tight-fitting lid as soon as possible to keep them from absorbing the oxygen from the air. These packets can be purchased from food storage companies (see Resource Guide for suggested sources).

Dry Ice Method

Another effective method of removing oxygen from food containers is to place a Mylar bag inside a plastic bucket. Add about 3 inches of food inside the Mylar bag then place a 3-inch square of dry ice on top of the food. Fill the bucket about half full and add another piece of dry ice. Fill the bucket full and allow thirty minutes to two hours for the ice to dissipate, forcing the oxygen out as it does so. Lay the lid on loosely so the gas produced by the dry ice can escape. Then seal the bucket tightly. One pound of dry ice is used for a 30-gallon drum of wheat, and one-sixth of a pound of dry ice is used for a 5-gallon bucket of wheat or grain. If the container bulges, take the lid off to let the gas out. Then seal the container again.

CO_2 or Nitrogen Flush Method

A method that you might use instead of the dry ice method is the CO_2 method (also called nitrogen flush). A welding shop will rent you a CO_2 tank and nitrogen gas. Just flush the food with the gas, making sure you get the hose down into the bottom of the container after the food has been put in it. Sometimes, especially when you're sealing containers of flour, the food can spray all over, so be careful.

Again, the nitrogen pack method and oxygen absorbers will remove the oxygen and prevent insects from living. Because they can't breathe without oxygen, the larvae die before they even hatch.

Bay Leaves Method

Placing bay leaves into your grain and spreading them throughout the container is another popular method of discouraging bug infestation. Because bugs don't like the smell of bay leaves, they are deterred from getting into the food. Two bay leaves per gallon or ten leaves spread throughout a 5-gallon bucket are enough to effectively do the job. Bay leaves laid inside storage cupboards will discourage bug infestation there as well.

Freezing Grain Method

If you live in an area where winter temperatures drop below freezing, you can probably kill any weevil that is present by placing your buckets of grain in an unheated garage or other storage area for the winter. You can also deep-freeze grain in 10-pound bags and leave it in your freezer for a week to kill any bugs. After you take the grain out of the freezer, if any moisture appears to have gotten into it, let the grain dry then seal it in the proper containers.

Diatomaceous Earth Method

You can also mix diatomaceous earth into your stored grains and beans to control insects without having to remove the dust before you consume the food. The diatomaceous earth you want to use is sold as an organic garden insecticide and is not harmful when ingested. *Warning:* There are several types of diatomaceous earth. Make sure you get the kind that is approved for human consumption rather than the swimming pool type, which contains harmful chemicals.

For every 40 pounds of grain or beans, mix one cup of diatomaceous earth with it. Mix it in small batches to be sure it coats every kernel. Cover your mouth and nose so you don't breathe the fine dust because it can irritate your lungs.

Using the Right Storage Containers

The very best way to protect your stored food is to start with the right food storage containers. They must be food-grade containers that will exclude light, oxygen, and moisture. Such containers will also protect your food from infestation of insects such as weevils and black sugar beetles.

Rotating Foods Regularly

Even if you successfully avoid bug infestation and prevent spoilage and deterioration, your food will eventually expire, much as people who avoid disease eventually succumb to old age. For that reason, it's important that you keep track of when you acquired the food and schedule regular rotation of each item, according to its shelf life expectancy.

This section will discuss the different types of storage containers available and how to properly remove the oxygen and seal them for long-term storage.

Plastic Buckets or Pails

An excellent method for storing food is to use buckets that have tight-fitting lids with rubber gaskets. Gaskets are necessary to prevent moisture or microscopic organisms from having access to the contents. Such buckets in 5- or 6-gallon sizes are ideal for large quantities of grains, legumes, sugar, flour, pasta, and similar items. *Note:* Never use buckets that have contained chemicals, paint, sheet rock mud, or other potentially toxic materials. Restaurant food-grade containers are okay if you first wash them well and them rinse with bleach and water. Buckets also can be purchased from a container company (refer to the Resource Guide for recommended companies).

Mylar Bags

You can purchase an inner liner that is made of metallized foil called Mylar. This liner will block out light that would otherwise harm the food and cause it to deteriorate. It also acts as a barrier that prevents moisture from entering and keeps rodents out. The metallized liner inserted into a 5- or 6-gallon bucket, and sealed properly with a tight-fitting lid, is a very good method of storing food.

After inserting the liner into a bucket, fill the bucket to about one inch below the top with the food you wish to store.

Carefully pull the liner up as tall as you can (it will be taller than the bucket) and seal it by pressing the top opening together with a hot iron. It is helpful to have two people to do this, one to hold the bucket and the other to seal the liner. When sealing the top of the liner, leave an opening the size of a vacuum cleaner hose. Remove as much air as possible by vacuuming it out, being careful that you don't suck food into your vacuum cleaner. When the air is removed and the bag appears to be vacuum-packed, remove the vacuum hose and seal the small opening with a hot iron. Because the liner is tall, you will need to roll the excess liner down into the bucket and then seal with a plastic lid.

The Mylar bag can be opened to remove some of the contents and then easily resealed by simply ironing the top of the liner together again.

Containers to Avoid

Do *not* use paint buckets or any other containers that were previously used to store or mix chemicals. Do *not* use garbage bags because they may be treated with pesticides that will eventually contaminate your food.

Now that you're familiar with where and how you can successfully store food, the next chapter will detail the various categories of food and nonfood items you might choose to stock in your store.

CHAPTER 5

Building Your Stockpile of Food and Other Necessities

EGINNING A comprehensive food storage program
is a daunting task, to say the least. For that reason, I
recommend you begin stocking your home grocery
store with basics that will enable you to survive during relatively short-term emergencies, and then gradually expand
your inventory until it includes the full array of food and other
items your family uses. This chapter is intended to familiarize you
with the variety of items you might stock in your home store,
grouped in several categories. The first two categories are bread
and soup.

We've all heard the saying, "You can't live by bread alone." I
have a philosophy that you *can* live on bread *and soup*. Soup, with
its endless combinations and variations, can be very hearty and
nutritious. If you have a variety of dehydrated soup mixes and
all the ingredients for baking bread, you can feed your family in a
crisis and survive well. I believe that the ingredients for soups and
breads should be high on the priority list of food that you store.
For that reason, I recommend you begin your food storage

program by collecting and storing the ingredients for these two food types.

Breads

If you store the basic ingredients for baking, you will be able to make a wide variety of breads. *Quick breads* include banana bread, poppy seed bread, applesauce bread, and zucchini bread. *Yeast breads* include white and whole wheat bread, bread sticks, scones, Native American fry bread, tortillas, rolls, and cinnamon rolls. *Dessert breads* include cakes, pie crust, and cookies. You can also make pancakes, waffles, biscuits, muffins, crackers, cornbread, dumplings, and even homemade noodles from flour and other basic ingredients. See chapter 8 for great recipes.

Ingredients for Baking

To be ready to make any of the bread types mentioned above, you'll need a wheat grinder, the necessary equipment for mixing and baking, and the basic ingredients listed here.

Ingredients for Breads

Staples
- [ ] Wheat for grinding
- [ ] White flour
- [ ] Cornmeal
- [ ] Oatmeal
- [ ] Powdered milk
- [ ] Dried whole eggs
- [ ] Baking powder
- [ ] Baking soda

- ☐ Salt
- ☐ Yeast

Spices and Flavorings
- ☐ Cinnamon
- ☐ Vanilla
- ☐ Baking cocoa
- ☐ Other spices and flavorings

Sweeteners
- ☐ White sugar
- ☐ Honey
- ☐ Brown sugar
- ☐ Maple syrup
- ☐ Other sweeteners

Fats and Oils
- ☐ Shortening
- ☐ Butter powder
- ☐ Margarine powder
- ☐ Shortening powder
- ☐ Olive or vegetable oil
- ☐ Other fats and oils

Extra Ingredients
- ☐ Raisins
- ☐ Dried fruits
- ☐ Other extras _____

To figure out how much of each ingredient you will need to yield a three-month supply of bread, start with a basic bread recipe such as the following.

Basic Bread Ingredients

(Makes 2 loaves)

$2^1/_2$ cups warm water

$2/_3$ cup powdered milk

4 tablespoons honey

1 tablespoon salt

$1/_3$ cup oil or melted shortening

2 tablespoons egg powder mixed with 2 tablespoons water
   (or 2 eggs)

2 packages active dry yeast (or 2 tablespoons dry
   bulk yeast)

$4^1/_2$ cups whole wheat flour

$2^1/_2$ to 4 cups white flour

If your family eats one loaf of bread per day, this recipe would feed you for two days. To determine the amount of each ingredient you will need to store in order to make enough bread to supply your family for three months, multiply the quantity of each ingredient by 45. To determine quantities needed for a full year, multiply by 180 (see table 4).

Of course, you will want to use your own family's favorite recipe (or recipes), calculate the amount of each ingredient according to what your own family will need and the amount of time for which you wish to be prepared. In other words, you will adapt this process to fit your own goals.

Soups, Sauces, and Spices

Soups are another versatile food type. Also included in this section are sauces and spices, which are often incorporated into soups to make them easier to prepare and more flavorful.

TABLE 4. Bread Ingredients for 2 Days, 3 Months, 1 Year

Ingredient	2-Day Supply	3-Month Supply (×45)	1-Year Supply (×180)
Powdered milk	$2/3$ cup	30 cups or $1^3/4$ gallons	120 cups or $6^1/2$ gallons
Honey	4 tablespoons	$11^1/4$ cups	45 cups or $2^3/4$ gallons
Salt	1 tablespoon	3 cups	12 cups
Oil	$1/3$ cup	15 cups	60 cups or $3^3/4$ gallons
Dried egg powder	2 tablespoons	6 cups	24 cups or $1^1/2$ gallons
Dried yeast	2 tablespoons	6 cups	24 cups or $1^1/2$ gallons
Whole wheat flour	$4^1/2$ cups	$202^1/2$ cups or $12^3/4$ gallons or $2^1/2$ (5-gallon) buckets	51 gallons or 10 (5-gallon) buckets
White flour	$2^1/2$ cups	$112^1/2$ cups or $7^1/2$ gallons or $1^1/2$ (5-gallon) buckets	30 gallons or 6 (5-gallon) buckets

Note: All measurements have been rounded off.

Dehydrated Soups

As I mentioned earlier, I feel that you can live on soup and bread. Storing dehydrated soups or soup ingredients is perhaps the best way to store the greatest amount of food in your available space. If you store all the dehydrated ingredients for making soup, you can make tasty, nutritious meals for your family. Here is a list of the basic ingredients you will need:

Basic Soup Ingredients

- ❏ Instant bouillon: beef and chicken
- ❏ Tomato powder
- ❏ Dried vegetables: broccoli, bell peppers, green beans, corn, carrots, celery, mushrooms, potatoes, cabbage, peas, and onions
- ❏ Grains and legumes: barley, rice, and beans
- ❏ TVP (textured vegetable protein): chicken-flavored and beef-flavored
- ❏ Pasta: ABC pasta (available through food storage companies), noodles, and others
- ❏ Spices: salt, pepper, parsley, garlic powder, onion powder, chili powder, and others
- ❏ Dairy: butter powder, powdered milk, cheddar cheese powder

Commercially Canned Soups

Canned soups that your family enjoys should be part of your emergency store. These soups are not only conveniently ready to eat, but can be used as the base for a large pot of soup. Some—such as cream of chicken and cream of mushroom—are also great to use as sauces to flavor casseroles and pasta dishes. Other favorite ready-to-eat soups can be stored. Keep in mind that canned goods need to be rotated within a two-year period.

Sauces, Gravies, and Spices

When putting together a food storage program, remember the sauces, spices, and flavorings. These ingredients make otherwise bland, basic foods appetizing. Bouillons and soup bases are very important for flavorings. They can be used for flavoring rice, beans, pasta, and as a base for sauces. See chapter 8 for great soup and sauce recipes.

Gravy mixes are also a practical item to store. They are delicious over rice, potatoes, pasta, and can be mixed with canned meat to make an excellent sauce.

Spices of all kinds should be stored as well. They last only a few years before they start to lose their flavor, so rotate your spices and use them up.

Staples

In addition to the flour and other staples you will be using to make bread and soups, several other basic food items should be high on your list of foods to store.

Grains

Wheat is the most common grain and main constituent of bread. It should have less than 10 percent moisture content and at least 15 percent protein content. Wheat stores better when it is in the wholeberry state. Once you crack or grind the wheat, it will lose nutrients more quickly and won't store as long as whole-berry wheat. I store white wheat (which is wonderful!) as well as red wheat. White wheat, by the way, is *not* the same as the white flour available at grocery stores (which is basically dead nutritionally because the wheat germ, bran, and endosperm have been removed in the milling process and the flour bleached). Instead, wheat white is a whole-kernel wheat form that is naturally white in color. You can grind it fresh to make white loaves of bread that are 100 percent whole wheat and highly nutritious. See the Resource Guide for recommended sources through which you can purchase white wheat.

I recommend that you stock your home grocery with a wide variety of grains. Do *not* store only wheat. If you or another family member should prove to be allergic to wheat, then you're likely to end up giving it away or taking it to the dump, thus wasting the money you spent on a large amount of wheat. Many different types of grains are available, including basics such as barley, buckwheat, corn, farina, germade, oats, rice, and rye; super grains such as amaranth, kamut, millet, quinoa, spelt, and triticale; and combinations such as six-grain and nine-grain blends.

Rice, Brown and White

Although brown rice is believed to have greater food value than white rice, it doesn't store very long—only three to six months. That's because the outer shell of the hull contains oil, which will become rancid. You can extend the shelf life of brown rice by keeping it in your freezer. I suggest that you use only white rice for long-term storage.

Pasta

Pasta will last about two years on the shelf. The many different types of pasta available include typical family favorites such as fettuccini, linguini, spaghetti, and various other noodles.

Of course, the real flavor in pasta dishes comes from the sauces. Make sure you store your favorites—Alfredo sauce mixes, canned soups, cheese sauce mixes, spaghetti sauce, and anything else that you use over pasta or rice.

Beans and Other Legumes

Another nutritious category of staple food is legumes. Again, a wide variety is available. You can store, for example, black beans, great northern beans, lentils, navy beans, pinto beans, or dried split and whole peas. Beans are a great source of protein; and when combined with rice, this staple product becomes a complete protein. Beans can be used whole, sprouted, or ground into bean flour to thicken sauces and gravies, as well as used as instant refried beans (see recipes in chapter 8). Rice and beans (and other legumes) are a great source of protein and can be used in place of meat. Add a little TVP (textured vegetable protein) to the recipe for great flavor and texture. TVP, a meat substitute made from soybeans, is discussed later in this chapter.

Protein Foods

Protein foods are sometimes overlooked in a food storage program simply because meats are expensive and it's harder to find meats that can be stored effectively over the long term. Yet because we require a certain amount of protein to remain in good health, it's important to stock protein-rich foods in your home grocery stores and to consume foods from this category regularly.

Canned Meats

I suggest you start with tuna and salmon in cans. Both are readily available, are generally popular with all family members, and are particularly rich in protein. Other items you might wish to stock include Spam, beef dices, beef stew, beef and rice, chicken dices, chicken chop suey, canned chicken, canned beef, canned ham, and canned sausage. Look for any other meat products that you might add to your other food storage items to make a good meal. For example, you might add canned ham to beans to make ham and beans. Tuna can be added to pasta to make a casserole. Beef chunks can be added to vegetables and spices to make stews. Chicken can be added to noodles to make chicken and noodles or chicken noodle soup.

Peanut Butter

Peanut butter is considered a protein food. It doesn't store as long as canned goods and dehydrated foods do because it contains oil, which can go rancid. Don't store more peanut butter than you can rotate within a year.

You can also purchase dehydrated peanut butter powder through food storage companies. However, it is generally used for baking (commercial bakeries often use it). When mixed with water so it can be used as a spread it is pretty bland and simply isn't as good as the real thing. You can improve the taste of dehydrated peanut butter by mixing a little vegetable oil with it.

Dehydrated Eggs

Dehydrated eggs are considered a protein food also. Dried eggs are great for long-term storage because you can use them in any recipe that calls for regular eggs. They taste the same as fresh eggs and can be cooked just like scrambled eggs and omelets. Unless you have chickens, you won't be able to get fresh eggs in an emergency situation. Because dried eggs are such a great alternative, I feel it's very important to store them.

Dried eggs last up to five years unopened, but must be used within one year after being opened. When I open a gallon-size can of dried eggs, I divide the eggs into four quart-size jars and keep them in the refrigerator as they are being used. Refer to the recipes in chapter 8 to learn how to use dried eggs.

Textured Vegetable Protein (TVP)

Textured vegetable protein comes in many flavors, such as barbeque, beef, chicken, pepperoni, plain, sausage, taco, and more. TVP, which is made from soybeans, is considered a meat substitute. In fact, TVP is made to resemble granules of ground meat;

when reconstituted, it looks like chopped beef or chicken. People on vegetarian diets can eat TVP. It is good in soups, stews, chili with beans, tacos, and as well as in recipes for main meals that call for (or include) meat or in dishes that need additional flavoring.

Be careful with any TVP that is heavily flavored. It very likely contains additives such as MSG (monosodium glutamate) and flavorings that can make some people sick. If you are sensitive to MSG (as I am), be aware that certain flavors of TVP contain MSG.

Fruits and Vegetables

A well-rounded diet includes both fruits and vegetables consumed on a daily basis. Fortunately, we have commercial access to both these major food categories in many forms that are easy to store. In addition, both can be home-grown and home-packaged for long-term storage.

Commercially Canned Fruits and Vegetables

Wet-pack commercially canned fruits—such as apple pie filling, applesauce, apricots, blueberries, cherries, fruit cocktail, mandarin oranges, peaches, pears, pineapple, and plums—are great for storage. Store your family's favorite canned fruits, making sure that you rotate them within two years.

Commercially canned vegetables are also ideal for storage. Typical family favorites include asparagus, carrots, green beans, mushrooms, mixed vegetables, onions, peas, potatoes, sweet corn, and tomatoes.

Commercially Dehydrated Foods

Most of us use dehydrated foods every day, whether we know it or not. These so-called "convenience foods" include items such as

Bisquick, gravy mixes, Hamburger Helper, instant oatmeal, instant soups such as Lipton Onion or Cup of Noodles, macaroni and cheese, Pasta Roni, powdered milk, Rice-a-Roni, Tuna Helper, and anything to which you "just add water."

Dehydrated foods are second only to fresh foods in nutrition value. They are processed using a high vacuum and low drying temperature, which removes most of the water. The product is typically brittle and hard rather than leathery like dried fruits.

Dehydrated foods, when harvested and preserved properly, will retain their vitamins, minerals, and enzymes. That's because the food has not been cooked or canned, which kills the enzymes

Advantages of Dehydrated Food

Dehydrated food weighs less and is much easier to store than wet-pack food. It also requires far less space than hydrated forms, easily fitting into cans and buckets; yet, when reconstituted, dehydrated food will yield at least double or triple its dry weight. It is also less expensive than wet-pack food because you aren't paying for all the water.

You can rehydrate dried food to restore it to its natural state. The taste is still great and the food value is excellent.

Dehydrated foods store well for long periods of time if properly canned (refer to methods of canning in chapter 6). Most dried food items keep for five to ten years, which is far longer than comparable foods that are wet-pack canned.

that are so vital to the digestive process. Despite its dried-up appearance, dehydrated food is actually "live" food.

Dehydrated Fruits

Dehydrated fruits are great for snacks and can be eaten dried or reconstituted and used just like the wet-pack fruits. Common favorites include apple bits, applesauce, apricots, banana slices, dates, figs, fruit mix, peach slices, peach- and strawberry-apple flakes, prunes, and raisins.

Dehydrated Vegetables

Dehydrated vegetables include bell peppers, broccoli florets, cabbage, carrot dices, celery, green beans, mushrooms, onions, potato dices, potato flakes, potato granules, potato pearls, sweet peas, sweet corn, tomato powder, and vegetable stew blend. Choose your favorites from all of these to make nutritious and tasty vegetable dishes. *Hint:* Dehydrated vegetables are great with cheese and other sauces.

Freeze-Dried Fruits and Vegetables

Freeze-dried fruits and vegetables are very similar to dehydrated. However, the water has all been taken out and they are much lighter in weight, which is the reason they are so popular with backpackers. Freeze-dried foods are more expensive than dehydrated foods because of the more complex process they go through to remove the water.

You can buy many of your family's favorite fruits in freeze-dried form. I've seen apples, blueberries, fruit mix, peaches, raspberries, and strawberries available for purchase.

A variety of freeze-dried vegetables (as well as meals) are also available commercially in foil packets. You can make a tasty vegetable meal by simply opening the package and reconstituting the contents by adding water.

Dairy Foods

Because dairy products are perishable, and might be difficult to get in an emergency situation, it's best to store them in dried form. Dry dairy products include butter powder, buttermilk powder, cheese blend, powdered chocolate milk, powdered milk, and sour cream powder. These are all available in the #10 (gallon-size) cans and can be stored for up to five years in a cool, dry place.

Fun Foods: Drinks, Boxed Mixes, and Condiments

I consider "fun foods" items such as candy, canned juices, dessert fillings, drink mixes, jams, jellies, Jell-O, ketchup, mayonnaise, olives, pickles, popcorn, pudding mixes, relishes, and salad dressing. Most people consider these "extras" and might not think of storing them, but they are a nice supplement to your food storage basics. If you had to live on your storage for very long, you would be grateful to have some fun items such as these to make your diet more interesting. Because I am addicted to popcorn, I store several cases of popcorn in #10 cans.

Storing Items for Special Family Members

It is important that you keep the special needs of the oldest and the youngest family members in mind when planning for long-term storage. A well-planned food storage program should allow for the feeding of babies and young children, as well as other family members. Care should be taken that a mother's diet is sufficient to permit her to nurse an infant as long as possible, which provides the best source of nutrients for the baby. Refer to the chapter 1 lists of suggested items for 72-hour packs for babies and for small children, including "other" items you have added to that list, and increase the amounts of each item as needed to meet your targeted supply.

Animals Need Food and Water, Too

Most people's animals are like children, totally dependent on them. We tend to become very upset when our animals are hurt, lost, or hungry, and would hate to see them starve. The simple solution is to store enough dry food for your animals for at least a three-month period of time.

Indoor Pets

Figure how much your dogs and cats eat in a week and multiply that amount by 12 to calculate a three-month supply. Or simply estimate how long a bag of food lasts and figure how many bags you'd need to feed each animal for the length of time you want your storage to last. For example, if it takes your dog approximately three weeks to eat a 50-pound bag of food, four bags should keep him fed for three months. I've read books that include recipes for making dog food. My opinion is this: If I am in a crisis situation, I'm not going to have time to make dog food.

Animals need good water also. Store a little extra for them, probably a pint a day per small dog or cat. Large dogs require about half a gallon per day. Even small animals such as hamsters, snakes, fish, and other pets that live indoors should be considered when planning food and water storage.

Birds become frightened during natural disasters. Your pet birds may fly away and get lost or hurt. Plan ahead of time what you would do with your birds in an emergency, and store enough bird food to last several months.

Outdoor Animals and Livestock
Animals such as horses, cows, chickens, goats, and other outdoor animals can also become frightened during a disaster. Be sure they have adequate shelter. Most people keep enough hay, alfalfa, and grain in storage during the winter months. Figure out how much you need to have on hand and plan accordingly.

Nonfood Items

Although your family is likely to be able to survive without most nonfood items, your quality of life would change drastically. Imagine, for example, life without toiletries and cleaning supplies! I recommend you also store any nonfood products that you regularly use so you would experience minimal disruption during an emergency situation. Nonfood items include all paper products (including toilet paper), cleansers, personal hygiene items, and other nonfood consumable goods. The following is a suggested list of items you might choose from. Add to it as necessary.

Nonfood Emergency Items

Paper Products
- ❏ Aluminum foil
- ❏ Matches
- ❏ Napkins
- ❏ Paper cups
- ❏ Paper plates
- ❏ Paper towels
- ❏ Plastic utensils

- ❏ Resealable plastic bags
- ❏ Toilet paper
- ❏ Trash bags
- ❏ Other _____

Personal Hygiene Items
- ❏ Sanitary napkins
- ❏ Shampoo and conditioner
- ❏ Shaving equipment
- ❏ Toothpaste and toothbrushes
- ❏ Towels and washcloths
- ❏ Other _____

Cleaners
- ❏ Bleach
- ❏ Cleanser
- ❏ Clothesline and clothespins
- ❏ Dish soap
- ❏ Hand soap
- ❏ Laundry soap
- ❏ Other _____

Personal Items
- ❏ Boots
- ❏ Brush and comb
- ❏ Coats
- ❏ Deodorant
- ❏ Facial moisturizer
- ❏ Gloves
- ❏ Hand lotion
- ❏ Hats

- ❏ Makeup
- ❏ Personal clothing
- ❏ Prescription glasses
- ❏ Sunblock
- ❏ Sunglasses
- ❏ Wool socks
- ❏ Other _____

Where to Get Foods for Storage

In the next chapter, you will read about cost-effective ways to obtain the various items you'll want to store. You'll also find a detailed inventory list in chapter 7, "Implementing Your Food Storage Program" to help you track your food and supplies as you accumulate them.

CHAPTER 6

Obtaining Food for Storage

S MENTIONED earlier, you do not need to put out a great deal of cash to stock your home grocery store. Not only can you do so by gradually adding just what you can afford, but you can actually *save money* and *avoid waste* by having your own store.

In addition, most food systems involve growing and preserving goods at home, or purchasing fruit and vegetables in season and "putting up" or canning these foods. Here are some ways you can save and avoid waste by stocking up on foods:

- Buy bulk and sale items.
- Plant your own garden and preserve what you grow.
- Sprout your own seeds and legumes.
- Dehydrate and home-can seasonal items.

Buying Commercial Products

Because you will be buying for the future rather than for the present, you have an ideal opportunity to wait for sales and seasonal specials. Also, because you will be buying for months at a time rather than just a week's worth as most consumers do, you have the opportunity to buy in bulk, which is almost always much less expensive. You can easily find commercial food (as well as non-food) products packaged in large containers or sold by the case at discounted prices.

People who store food for emergencies frequently buy directly from food growers, through restaurant or grocery suppliers, and through food storage companies, as well as take advantage of discount warehouse buys. By buying in bulk, you can usually get what you need at greatly reduced prices. Because many of the food storage companies listed in the Resource Guide specialize in packaging foods in bulk, I recommend you check out what they have available.

Anticipate your needs for a three-month period of time. Buy bulk food in larger quantities and store it in plastic food-grade buckets that have airtight lids, or purchase food that's already been sealed properly in buckets or #10 cans.

Doing Simple Gardening

There's nothing more satisfying than eating what you've grown yourself. Besides, fresh fruits and vegetables are better for your health than anything else you could buy. Anything live still has all the enzymes and nutrients in the food. For that reason, I recommend you store garden seeds and get in the habit of growing your own food if you possibly can. Not only can you enjoy fresh vegetables and fruit, but you can home-can or dehydrate what you produce for future use and emergency storage. In addition, if you were not able to buy food following an emergency situation, you could continue feeding your family by planting a garden and producing your own food.

Even if you don't have a large outdoor area for a big garden plot, you can usually find space in a small yard, in pots or boxes on a patio or deck, or even indoors to grow at least some fresh items. If nothing else, you can sprout your own seeds, beans, and other legumes (see instructions later in this chapter) so you can always have something fresh to eat.

Gardening Tools

It is important to have sufficient tools on hand to plant and cultivate your garden. The following is a general list of gardening equipment and tools you will need to grow a garden.

Gardening Needs

- ❏ Garden hose
- ❏ Hand tools
- ❏ Hoe or cultivator
- ❏ Pick
- ❏ Poles or rigid square fencing for pole beans
- ❏ Rake
- ❏ Shovel
- ❏ Stakes to mark rows
- ❏ String to mark rows
- ❏ Tiller
- ❏ Tomato cages
- ❏ Wheelbarrow
- ❏ Other _____

Once you've done some gardening, you'll probably want to add other items to the above equipment list.

Locating Your Garden Plot

Although it is nice to have a large area of tilled land in the sun for your garden plot, that isn't necessary. If you live on a small piece of land and do not have an existing place to grow a garden, you can till up some of your yard or use existing flower beds. If you plan your garden right, you can produce a lot of food in a small place. Vegetables can even be grown in window boxes, on porches, or in window sills. Grow tomatoes, beans, cucumbers, and squash on poles or fences—and tie them up to save space.

Once you have selected a garden spot, till under the old leftover plants or vegetation. Remove all weeds and dispose of them. Rake the area so it is smooth and free of rocks, twigs, and other debris.

Organic compost, topsoil, or other types of mulch should be worked into the soil so it is not compacted or hard like clay. The soil is best when it is loose and full of nutrients from compost or mulch (see instructions on composting). This will allow the water to seep all the way to the roots of the plants.

To plant, follow the directions on the seed packages. Plant the rows far enough apart so that you can till under any weeds that come up between the rows. If the weeds are killed while they are young, you won't have them taking over your garden. We have found that by weeding our garden every week for about a month, most of the weeds will be gone, and the rest of the growing season will be nearly weed free. Be sure to water your plants often, or they will dry out and die.

Grow Boxes

Grow boxes are a great gardening option. You can easily build one yourself by choosing a plot of ground then using four 12-foot and four 4-foot boards of 2 × 6 (2-inch by 6-inch) lumber to build a rectangular box that's 12 feet long, 4 feet wide, and 12 inches high.

Simply put two 12-foot boards on top of each other for the length and two 4-foot boards on top of each other for each side (see figure 6.1). Secure them by nailing to wooden stakes at each corner. Fill the boxes with topsoil.

You can plant a lot of food in just one grow box. You'll also find that less water is needed to irrigate these relatively small growing areas, and that it's easier to pull out weeds and harvest plants from the raised beds.

My husband and I plant carrots in one of our grow boxes, and when it gets cold in the fall, we leave the carrots in the ground, cover the box with a tarp, and cover the tarp with leaves. This keeps our carrots from freezing, and we can enjoy eating them in the springtime. They stay as fresh and crisp as they were in the fall.

We also plant grow boxes with vegetables that will come up again in the spring, such as small onions, chives, herbs, Swiss chard, mustard greens, and spinach. We cut the greens just above the root and leave the root in the grow box for the winter. Then in the spring, the vegetables pop up again when it starts to get warm.

Figure 6.1 Grow boxes are a great gardening option.

Greenhouses

A greenhouse is nice to have if you want to be self-sufficient, because you get a longer growing season inside a greenhouse (see figure 6.2). You can start plants growing early in the springtime and keep them growing long after the usual fall harvest.

You can start the following seeds either indoors or in a greenhouse: broccoli, Brussels sprouts, cabbage, cauliflower, celery, cucumbers, eggplant, melons, peppers, tomatoes, and others. Your tomatoes will grow better if you start them at least two months before you plant them in the garden.

Indoor Gardening

Indoor gardening can be done in window sills, hanging pots, planters, and other containers. Indoor mini-gardens can be set up using trays. It's even possible to grow plants in unlighted areas, such as your basement or garage. Grow lights are available to give plants the much-needed light when sunlight doesn't reach them.

Figure 6.2 A greenhouse provides you with a longer growing season.

Storing and Planting Garden Seeds

Hybrid seeds can be purchased and used from year to year, but they do not reproduce seeds that you can save. I've successfully grown plants from garden seeds I've kept for as long as five years. However, as seeds get older, they are less likely to germinate. I recommend you use the freshest seeds you can get, for best results. For long-term emergencies, nonhybrid seeds will reproduce, and you can save the seeds from year to year and use them if you can't get any others.

The following basic seeds are good for growing in most climates: asparagus, broccoli, Brussels sprouts, beets, cabbage, cantaloupe, cucumbers, eggplant, endive, green onions, kale, kohlrabi, lettuce, melons, mustard greens, okra, pole or bush beans, parsley, parsnips, peas, peppers, pumpkin, radish, rutabaga, spinach, squash, sweet corn, Swiss chard, tomato, turnips, and watermelon.

Follow the specific directions for planting that you'll find on the back of each seed packet. I also recommend that you check with your local garden nursery to find out which vegetables grow best in your climate.

Composting

"Compost" is anything that will decompose, such as leftover fruit and vegetable peelings, coffee grounds, grass clippings, leaves, egg shells, garden vegetables that don't get used or go rotten, as well as apples and other fruit that falls from the trees and doesn't get used.

All these items (and others that will decompose) can be put into a pit or a large wooden box. Rotate the mixture every few weeks with a pitchfork or shovel. Within a couple of months, it will be ready for use. You can then mix this compost with topsoil, mulch, rabbit droppings, or manure. It makes a great soil for planting. It can also enrich the soil in your grow boxes. Just mix the compost with other topsoil, fill your grow boxes, and plant seeds in them. Because gardening takes some level of skill, I suggest that you read a book on the subject before you try it. Many good books on gardening and composting are available through the companies listed in the Resource Guide. You can also find excellent books on the subject in any large bookstore.

Sprouting Seeds and Legumes

Sprouting—growing bean sprouts and alfalfa sprouts, for example—provides an excellent source of nutrition. Sprouts will give you the enzymes (see sidebar for more about enzymes) and nutrients that you would normally get by eating fresh fruits and vegetables. That's because sprouts not only retain their enzymes, but after sprouting, their vitamins and minerals increase by at least 75 percent. I believe that sprouting seeds are almost as vital to food storage as water and that they probably should be among your first long-term storage investments.

These seeds are different from the ones you use to plant your garden. The following seeds and legumes are available specifically for sprouting: alfalfa, broccoli, lentils, radish, red clover, salad blends, sprouting peas, sunflower, wheat, and legumes such as adzuki, garbanzo, kidney, mung, pinto, red, and soybeans. The seeds should be untreated and should not be sealed in airtight or nitrogen-packed containers. They need to breathe air to keep them alive. If you plan to sprout wheat to make wheatgrass, label the bucket so you know that it is wheat for sprouting rather than for baking. These sprouting seeds will die and won't sprout if they are nitrogen-packed or sealed with an oxygen packet.

Sprouts are best when eaten raw—in salads, on sandwiches, or added to stir-frys *after* cooking. Cooking the sprouts kills the enzymes, which are vital to our health.

The Importance of Enzymes

Enzymes are found in fresh foods that have not been heated or cooked in any way. The enzymes aid the body in digestion of food, including protein floating around in the blood. Enzymes are essential to our health and are plentiful in fresh fruits and vegetables. When fresh foods are not readily available, sprouts are a great alternative to garden-fresh produce. Because it takes relatively little space and light to grow sprouts, you can consider your sprouting area an effective indoor garden.

It's good to have on hand about one pound of sprouting seeds per person per month.

Storing Your Sprouting Seeds

It's best if you can purchase your sprouting seeds fresh each year. However, if you plan to store seeds for a long time, be sure you take great care to ensure that your seeds can breathe. As these seeds sit dormant, they give off carbon dioxide. Therefore, they need to be freshened up by being poured out of the container or stirred up to introduce new oxygen into the container at least once each year.

How to Sprout

You do need to learn how to grow sprouts properly. First, you need to have quart jars and sprouting trays, which are available commercially (see Resource Guide). To grow sprouts successfully, follow these steps:

Step One: Clean. Sort through beans or seeds to make sure they are clean and free of dirt clots and broken pieces.

Step Two: Rinse. Rinse the beans or seeds by placing them in a wide-mouth quart jar with a plastic lid with holes for drainage. (Instead of a plastic lid, you can use fabric, nylon netting, or plastic screen material secured with an elastic band around the mouth of the jar.) Fill the jar with water and then pour the rinse water out.

Step Three: Soak. Fill the jar with water again and soak for the number of hours specified in table 5. Lukewarm purified drinking water is the best—or distilled water from the grocery store. You want to avoid chlorinated or salt-softened water.

Step Four: Drain. Drain all the soaking water from the jar. The water should *not* be foamy; if it is, the beans (or seeds) have started to ferment.

Step Five: Grow. Beans and seeds can be sprouted in the jars in which they are soaked or in sprouting trays (trays work best for beans, sunflower seeds, and buckwheat). If you are using a sprouting tray, pour the beans or seeds evenly onto the bottom of the tray. Cover with a lid or dishcloth. Place the tray or jar in a warm place; sprouts do best at a temperature of 65 to 80 degrees F. Rinse twice a day and drain off all excess water. It generally takes between three to five days to grow sprouts (see table 5).

Step Six: Expose to Sunlight. As the sprouts mature, they can be moved to a window sill for a few hours or in direct sunlight to develop the green color or chlorophyll.

Step Seven: Harvest and Eat. Bean sprouts are best eaten when the sprout is popping its head out of the seed. Other seeds are best when doubled in size. When sprouts are ready, put them in a container of water to rinse off the hulls or leftover seeds. You can keep them in your refrigerator in airtight plastic bags for a few days. If sprouts are kept more than a week in the refrigerator, however, they may go sour. Eat them up quickly!

Step Eight: Freeze for Stir-Fry Dishes. Sprouts can be frozen and used in stir-fry dishes later. Place them in plastic bags and seal them airtight before freezing.

Sprouting Times

The various types of sprouting seeds require different lengths of time for soaking and sprouting, as well as yield different amounts when mature. Table 5 details the variations in the most common types of sprouting seeds and beans.

Wheatgrass Tonic

Wheatgrass must be sprouted on trays with topsoil about 1/2-inch thick. Since it takes some skill to grow wheatgrass, I recommend that you read up on growing it. You can purchase a good book on the subject in almost any large bookstore, or look up "wheatgrass" or "sprouting" on the Web. Once you get the hang of growing wheatgrass, you can put it through a wheatgrass juicer and make a very healthful tonic. Wheatgrass juice is full of chlorophyll and enzymes, as well as vitamins and minerals. Because this tonic can act as a laxative if you are not accustomed to it, I recommend you take only about one ounce per day to start.

TABLE 5. Sprouting Chart

Seed	Amount	Soaking Time	Sprouting Time	Volume
Alfalfa	2 tablespooons	4 hours	5 to 7 days	2 cups
Buckwheat	$1/2$ cup	12 hours	2 to 3 days	$2^1/2$ cups
Cabbage	2 tablespoons	4 to 6 hours	3 to 4 days	$1/2$ cup
Clover	2 tablespoons	4 to 6 hours	3 to 5 days	$1/2$ cup
Fenugreek	$1/2$ cup	12 hours	4 to 5 days	2 cups
Garbanzo	$1/2$ cup	12 hours	2 to 3 days	2 cups
Lentil	$1/2$ cup	12 hours	3 to 4 days	2 cups
Mung Beans	$1/2$ cup	12 hours	3 to 4 days	2 cups
Mustard	2 tablespoons	4 to 6 hours	3 to 4 days	2 cups
Pinto Beans	$1/2$ cup	12 hours	3 to 5 days	$1^1/2$ cups
Pumpkin	$1/2$ cup	12 hours	3 to 5 days	2 cups
Quinoa	$1/2$ cup	4 hours	3 to 5 days	2 cups
Radish	2 tablespoons	4 to 6 hours	3 to 4 days	2 cups
Soybeans	$1/2$ cup	12 hours	3 to 4 days	2 cups
Sunflower	$1/2$ cup	12 hours	3 to 4 days	4 cups
Triticale	$1/2$ cup	12 hours	4 to 5 days	$1^1/2$ cups
Wheat (for wheatgrass)	1 cup	12 hours	5 days	3 cups

The actual length of sprouting time varies depending on specific conditions under which the sprouts are grown. You will have to experiment a little and get a feel for when your sprouts are ready to eat. Sprouts will expand at least four times their dry volume. However, it's best to eat them when they have doubled in size.

Dehydrating Foods at Home

Food dehydration is the process of removing moisture from food using warm air for evaporation. Some items, especially herbs, can be sun-dried with great success. Or you can purchase a home food dehydrator with controlled ventilation. The result is delicious dehydrated fruits, vegetables, and meats that you can store and eat later.

You can, for example, make raisins from grapes and prunes from plums. Other fruits that dry well are apples, apricots, bananas, dates, figs, papaya, pears, and pineapple. Vegetables that dehydrate well include bell peppers, green beans, onions, peas, squash, sweet corn, tomatoes, zucchini, and many others. Herbs such as basil, dill, mint, parsley, and so on are easily dried for long-term storage. Beef is often dehydrated to make beef jerky.

If you purchase a food dehydrator, it will come with complete instructions on how to dehydrate foods at home. You also should be able to find many good books on home dehydrating by asking at your local bookstore. Realize, however, that dehydrating your own three-month supply of food is not easily done. Unlike buying commercially dehydrated products, where all the work has been done for you, home dehydrating is very time-consuming.

Reconstituting Guidelines for Dehydrated Foods

When food is dehydrated, the water is evaporated out and the cell walls collapse. Some products, such as tomatoes, cannot be reconstituted to the texture that they were before. However, they can be used in soups, sauces, or seasonings.

It's very easy to reconstitute food. A good rule of thumb for reconstituting fruits, vegetables, and meats is to add about three times the amount of boiling water to the dry product and let it sit for at least twenty minutes. If you use cold water, the product must sit in the refrigerator for about four hours or overnight. If you have added too much water, you can drain it and use it in cooking. If it looks like you used too little water, then simply add more. If using commercially packaged items, follow package directions when they're listed. (See "Product Reconstitution Chart" in chapter 8.)

To speed up the reconstitution process, add the dried products directly to soup and cook as usual.

Home Canning Foods

Part of living providently is to "put up," or can, any excess fruits, vegetables, and meats from your garden and farm. Most people stock up on food during harvest in the fall and early winter. You will find that families in general are better prepared in the late fall or early winter than in the spring and summer. It is a natural thing to stock up with food as winter approaches, then to deplete it through the winter and spring.

Home canning is an art, but you can easily acquire this skill if you are willing to learn and have the right equipment. I suggest you get one of the many great books written on home canning and try it yourself. Fruits and tomatoes are probably the easiest to put up so I recommend you begin with those. Salsas, mixed vegetables, stews, soup, and meats are a little trickier. Get recipes that have been tested by a university extension service and are fairly recent. Be careful with recipes that have been handed down with directions changed in some way. You don't want to risk a bacterial infection from eating improperly processed or inadequately sealed canned food.

Vegetables that can be "put up" or canned at home include beets, carrots, corn, green beans, onions, peas, potatoes, squash, pumpkin, and turnips. You can also can whole tomatoes, tomato sauce, tomato juice, salsa, pickles, and relishes.

All fish and meats can be canned at home. Beef, chicken, deer, elk, grouse, pheasant, rabbit, salmon, tuna, and many others are often canned. Families that catch their own fish often home-can part of what they catch for future use. Families that include hunters typically obtain meat in the fall and winter months, when the wild game season is on, and can what they don't eat fresh. Lots of families raise cows, pigs, chickens, and other animals, and slaughter them during the cooler months. You can store these hunted or home-grown sources of protein for the long term by canning, freezing, or dehydrating them.

Fruits that are commonly canned at home include apples, apricots, cherries, peaches, and pears. People who home-can frequently put up items such as applesauce, grape and other fruit juices or nectars, and jams and jellies.

For convenience, keep all your canning equipment together and store it where you can easily find what you need when you need it. I had a special shelf built above my food storage shelves in my utility room where I now keep all my canning equipment—in fresh plastic garbage bags so it stays clean from one canning season to another.

The following is a list of equipment that you will need for home canning.

Canning Equipment

- ❏ Pint- and quart-size glass jars
- ❏ Metal rings and lids
- ❏ Jar lifter
- ❏ Boiling water bath canner
- ❏ Steam canner
- ❏ Pressure cooker with gauge
- ❏ Tomato strainer or grinder

- ❏ Juice steamer
- ❏ Large pot or kettle
- ❏ Wooden spoons
- ❏ Cooking utensils
- ❏ Bowls
- ❏ Other _____

You can purchase any of this canning equipment from many of the food storage companies listed in the Resource Guide.

To make the hard work of canning go much more quickly and easily, you might want to join one of the food storage groups that often get together to can food.

Now that you've read about where and how you can successfully store food for the long term, what items you might include in your food storage program, and how you might obtain those items, the next chapter will focus on putting all this information together to implement your plan.

CHAPTER 7

Implementing Your Food Storage Program

ow that you have an overview of the entire home
storage process, it's time to pull everything together
and implement your plan. This chapter will provide
you with the tools to effectively stock and maintain
inventory in your own home store.

Planning Your Food Storage Program

Just as storekeepers must purchase goods and continually manage
inventory so they don't overstock or run out of items, you will
have to carefully plan your food storage so you will always have
what you need when you need it. You can maintain well-stocked
shelves that will sustain your family by diligently applying the following rules:

1. Plan your food storage well and purchase it in a systematic and orderly fashion to avoid panic buying.

2. Avoid borrowing money or putting your purchases on your credit card if you don't have the means to pay it back promptly.

3. Budget carefully and shop wisely when items are on sale so you can save money.

4. Buy only what you know your family will eat so you don't waste money on food that won't be eaten.

5. Rotate food on a regular basis by replacing the items you use with new items.

6. Keep your food inventory list handy and mark the items as you use them so they can be replaced.

7. Use a marker to write on the containers what each item is, when it was purchased, and when it needs to be used.

Taking Action

Once you have budgeted funds for your family's food storage program, have chosen and prepared your home store location, and determined exactly what your family needs for the months ahead, it's time to begin stocking your store. As with any large, daunting task, this one will become easier when divided into smaller tasks that you can accomplish one at a time. Stocking your home store in logical sections is similar to writing a chapter at a time until an entire book is finished. The chart below divides the process into ten steps that you can focus on individually, perhaps one or two each month, until you have a full supply of food, nonfood items, and medical supplies to sustain your family in a crisis.

Because gathering a year's supply of the full range of foods you use is an extremely time-consuming and expensive project, I recommend you do it in stages. Start by putting together a three-month well-rounded supply rather than immediately gathering a year's supply of basics such as wheat, beans, rice, powdered milk, and honey. Although the basics are important, they are just the beginning of a balanced, palatable diet that will truly sustain your family. After you have completed your three-month supply, do it all over again to get a six-month supply, then again for a nine-month supply, then again until you've collected a full year's supply.

The following chart lists recommendations for tasks to complete and items to obtain, but it is only a guideline. Do *not* follow it exactly. You must prepare your own inventory and planning chart according to your own family's likes and what they eat now.

To be prepared, every family needs its own grocery store. By following this program, you too can be prepared within six months. Do it smart with a plan; but most important, "DO IT"!

Ten Steps to Family Preparedness: A Plan of Action

Step #1: Organize
- Prepare space in your home
- Build shelves and organize
- Create a 1-week menu
- Take inventory

Step #2: Water, Survival Equipment, and Gardening Needs
- Water
- Basic survival equipment
- Cooking equipment and fuel
- Garden seeds
- Sprouting seeds

Step #3: Medical Supplies and Special Needs
- Pharmacy and medical supplies
- Baby food and supplies (if applicable)
- Pet food and supplies (if applicable)

Step #4: Basic Ingredients for Baking
- Basic baking needs
- Sweeteners
- Fats
- Basic spices and flavorings

Step #5: Soups, Sauces, and Spice Mixes
- Canned soups
- Dehydrated soups
- Sauces and spice mixes

Step #6: Staples
- Cereals
- Rice
- Grains
- Legumes
- Pastas

Step #7: Protein Foods and Dried Dairy
- Commercial and home-canned meats
- Textured vegetable protein (TVP)
- Peanut butter
- Dehydrated eggs
- Dried dairy

Step #8: Fruits and Vegetables
- Commercial and home-canned fruits
- Dehydrated fruits
- Commercial and home-canned vegetables
- Dehydrated vegetables

Step #9: Fun Foods
- Dry drink mixes
- Canned drinks
- Desserts
- Boxed mixes
- Condiments
- Additional spices

Step #10: Nonfood Items
- Paper products
- Cleansers
- Personal hygiene

Planning Guide

Now that you have an overview of the items to store, it's time to create your own family's personalized list. As stated before, it's important that you tailor your plan to your family's needs and plan meals and menus based on your family's preferences.

Tailor Your Plan to Your Family's Needs

Your inventory list should include only what you know your family will eat. Don't use your parents', sister's, brother's, or neighbors' lists. To create your own list, you'll need to begin by coming up with menus that include all your favorite recipes and your family's favorite fun foods. Select only those products your own family eats now and slowly introduce any products you plan to store that they are not accustomed to eating.

Be sure this list is for the entire family. As we discussed before, young children and older people have a particularly hard time adjusting to eating only the basic food items such as wheat, beans, honey, and powdered milk.

Plan Your Meals and Menus

Start by planning out one week of complete menus (using the menu charts beginning on page 115), including between-meal snacks, and list all the ingredients used for every recipe. These are your "buffer" foods—those that will get you by for a short-term crisis without having to change your family's diet.

When you are finished with one week of menus, use table 6 on page 122 to calculate how much you will need of each ingredient. You will multiply the total amount of each ingredient used by twelve to determine how much of each item you will need to store for a three-month, well-rounded food storage program.

Sunday

Recipes Used	Ingredients Needed
BREAKFAST	
LUNCH	
DINNER	

Monday

Recipes Used	Ingredients Needed
BREAKFAST	
LUNCH	
DINNER	

Tuesday

Recipes Used	Ingredients Needed

BREAKFAST

LUNCH

DINNER

Wednesday

Recipes Used	Ingredients Needed

BREAKFAST

LUNCH

DINNER

Thursday

Recipes Used	Ingredients Needed
BREAKFAST	
LUNCH	
DINNER	

Friday

Recipes Used	Ingredients Needed

BREAKFAST

LUNCH

DINNER

Saturday

Recipes Used	Ingredients Needed
BREAKFAST	
LUNCH	
DINNER	

TABLE 6. Itemized Ingredients for 1-Week Menu Plan

Ingredient	Amount Needed for 1 Week	Amount Needed for 3 Months (× 12)

TABLE 6. Itemized Ingredients for 1-Week Menu Plan

Ingredient	Amount Needed for 1 Week	Amount Needed for 3 Months (× 12)

TABLE 6. Itemized Ingredients
for 1-Week Menu Plan

Ingredient	Amount Needed for 1 Week	Amount Needed for 3 Months (× 12)

Taking Inventory

The next step in your food storage program is to take inventory. It is important that you determine just how much of each item on your list you currently have in your cupboards or other food storage areas. The more accurate you are in taking inventory of the items you currently have on hand, the easier it will be for you to complete your program.

The following steps will help you complete your inventory:

1. Study the inventory-planning chart beginning on page 126 carefully so you are familiar with the different categories for food and nonfood items.

2. Go through your entire house, garage, basement, and any other locations where you have stored food or nonfood items. Count all case goods, dehydrated food cans, and other containers and write these figures (in pencil) in the "Amount on Hand" column. Although this is a time-consuming job, it is important that you do it before you begin purchasing additional items, to avoid overstocking and unnecessary spending.

3. If any items that your family uses are not on the inventory-planning chart, use the blank lines at the bottom of each product category to add them. If you need more space, attach a separate piece of paper.

4. Determine the amounts you'll need of each item for three months, using table 6 or other estimates. Subtract what you have on hand to determine what you need to purchase.

5. Update your chart as you made additions to your stock. When you have a three-month supply of an item, highlight that item with a yellow highlighter to show that you have completed it. Continue this process to complete a six-month and then one-year supply.

Inventory-Planning Chart

Water, Survival Equipment, and Gardening Needs		
Item	Amount on Hand	Amount Needed for 3 Months for Individual
Water		
Water		
Water containers		
Water purifier		
Basic Survival Equipment Shelter and Clothing Needs		
Blankets		
Coats		
Duct tape		
Hammer		
Large tent with repair kit		
Long underwear, insulated		
Pillows		
Plastic sheeting, 25 by 6 feet (4-millimeter thickness)		
Plastic tarp, 10 by 12 feet (waterproof)		
Pocket knife		
Rope, 150 feet		
Sheets		
Sleeping bags		
Warm clothing		

Amount Needed for 3 Months for Family (multiply individual amount by number of family members)	Amount Needed for 6 Months for Family (multiply 3-month amount by 2)	Amount Needed for 1 Year for Family (multiply 6-month amount by 2)

(continues)

Inventory-Planning Chart

Water, Survival Equipment, and Gardening Needs		
Item	Amount on Hand	Amount Needed for 3 Months for Individual
Warm hats and gloves		
Waterproof boots or warm shoes		
Wool socks		
Lighting Needs		
Butane igniter or cigarette lighter		
Candles with holders		
Flashlights with extra batteries and bulbs		
Gas or kerosene lanterns and fuel		
Liquid paraffin or 100-hour candles		
Waterproof matches and regular wooden matches		
Communication Needs		
Battery-powered spotlight		
Cell phone		
Flares		
Ham radio		
Portable radio and extra batteries		

Amount Needed for 3 Months for Family (multiply individual amount by number of family members)	Amount Needed for 6 Months for Family (multiply 3-month amount by 2)	Amount Needed for 1 Year for Family (multiply 6-month amount by 2)

(continues)

Inventory-Planning Chart

Water, Survival Equipment, and Gardening Needs		
Item	Amount on Hand	Amount Needed for 3 Months for Individual
Solar-powered battery charger and rechargeable batteries		
Walkie-talkies		
Gardening Needs		
Garden hose		
Hand tools		
Hoe or cultivator		
Pick		
Poles or rigid square fencing for pole beans		
Rake		
Shovel		
Stakes to mark rows		
String to mark rows		
Tiller		
Tomato cages		
Wheelbarrow		
Equipment for Cutting Wood		
Axes		
Bar chain oil		

Amount Needed for 3 Months for Family (multiply individual amount by number of family members)	Amount Needed for 6 Months for Family (multiply 3-month amount by 2)	Amount Needed for 1 Year for Family (multiply 6-month amount by 2)

(continues)

Inventory-Planning Chart

Water, Survival Equipment, and Gardening Needs		
Item	Amount on Hand	Amount Needed for 3 Months for Individual
Bow saw		
Chain saw with extra chains and spark plugs		
Engine starting fluid		
Gasoline		
Heavy leather gloves		
Measuring cup		
Oil and fuel mixing can		
Safety goggles		
Wood-splitting maul		
Cooking Equipment and Fuel		
Blender		
Bucket openers		
Buckets and lids		
Can opener		
Canning equipment		
Dehydrator		
Dish towels and rags		
Dutch ovens		
Electric grain mill		
Firewood		
Frying pans		
Hand grain mill		

Amount Needed for 3 Months for Family (multiply individual amount by number of family members)	Amount Needed for 6 Months for Family (multiply 3-month amount by 2)	Amount Needed for 1 Year for Family (multiply 6-month amount by 2)

(continues)

Inventory-Planning Chart

Water, Survival Equipment, and Gardening Needs		
Item	Amount on Hand	Amount Needed for 3 Months for Individual
Juicer		
Kitchen knives		
Ladles		
Measuring cups		
Metal grate for fire		
Mixer		
Pots and pans		
Pressure cooker		
Propane		
Propane cook stove		
Spatulas		
Sprouting Equipment		
Vacuum sealer		
Garden Seeds		
Banana squash		
Barley		
Beets		
Cabbage		
Carrots		

Amount Needed for 3 Months for Family (multiply individual amount by number of family members)	Amount Needed for 6 Months for Family (multiply 3-month amount by 2)	Amount Needed for 1 Year for Family (multiply 6-month amount by 2)

(continues)

Inventory-Planning Chart

Water, Survival Equipment, and Gardening Needs		
Item	Amount on Hand	Amount Needed for 3 Months for Individual
Celery		
Cucumbers		
Garden peas		
Onions		
Potatoes		
Spinach		
Summer squash		
Sweet corn		
Tomatoes		
Sprouting Seeds		
Alfalfa seeds		
Broccoli seeds		
Garbanzo beans		
Lentils		
Mung beans		
Pumpkin seeds		
Radish seeds		
Red clover seeds		
Salad mix seeds		
Soybeans		
Sunflower seeds		

Amount Needed for 3 Months for Family (multiply individual amount by number of family members)	Amount Needed for 6 Months for Family (multiply 3-month amount by 2)	Amount Needed for 1 Year for Family (multiply 6-month amount by 2)

(continues)

Inventory-Planning Chart

Medical Supplies and Special Needs		
Item	Amount on Hand	Amount Needed for 3 Months for Individual
Pharmacy and Medical Supplies		
Acetaminophen (Tylenol)		
Adhesive bandages		
Adhesive tape		
Antibiotic ointment		
Antibiotic, powered		
Aspirin		
Asthma inhaler (if applicable)		
Boric acid		
Butterfly closures		
Cold and cough medications		
Cotton balls and swabs		
Diarrhea remedy		
Elastic bandages		
Epsom salt		
First-aid book		
Gauze pads, assorted sizes		
Hot-water bottle		
Ibuprofen		
Instant heat and cold packs		
Iodine		
Ipecac syrup		
Laxatives		
Lip balm		

Amount Needed for 3 Months for Family (multiply individual amount by number of family members)	Amount Needed for 6 Months for Family (multiply 3-month amount by 2)	Amount Needed for 1 Year for Family (multiply 6-month amount by 2)

(continues)

Inventory-Planning Chart

Medical Supplies and Special Needs		
Item	Amount on Hand	Amount Needed for 3 Months for Individual
Milk of magnesia		
Needle and thread		
Ointments		
Personal medications		
Petroleum jelly		
Plastic spoons		
Rubbing alcohol		
Safety pins		
Scissors, small		
Splints (Popsicle sticks or tongue depressors)		
Sunblock		
Sunglasses		
Thermometer		
Triangular bandages		
Tweezers		
Vitamins		
Baby Food and Supplies (if applicable)		
Baby bath		
Baby cereal		
Baby juices		
Baby lotion		

Amount Needed for 3 Months for Family (multiply individual amount by number of family members)	Amount Needed for 6 Months for Family (multiply 3-month amount by 2)	Amount Needed for 1 Year for Family (multiply 6-month amount by 2)

Inventory-Planning Chart

Medical Supplies and Special Needs		
Item	Amount on Hand	Amount Needed for 3 Months for Individual
Baby medication		
Baby shampoo		
Blanket		
Bottles with nipples		
Canned baby food		
Diaper rash ointment		
Diapers and pins		
Disposable diapers		
Evaporated milk		
Extra clothing		
Formula		
Karo syrup		
Moist towelettes		
Toys		
Pet Food and Supplies (if applicable)		
Dry cat food		
Dry dog food		
Other pet food		

Amount Needed for 3 Months for Family (multiply individual amount by number of family members)	Amount Needed for 6 Months for Family (multiply 3-month amount by 2)	Amount Needed for 1 Year for Family (multiply 6-month amount by 2)

(continues)

Inventory-Planning Chart

Basic Ingredients for Baking		
Item	Amount on Hand	Amount Needed for 3 Months for Individual
Basic Baking Needs		
Baking powder*		
Baking soda*		
Buttermilk powder*		
Cornmeal*		
Cornstarch*		
Cream of tartar		
Dried whole eggs*		
Oatmeal*		
Powdered milk*		
Wheat for grinding*		
White flour*		
Yeast		
Sweeteners		
Brown sugar*		
Corn syrup		
Honey		
Maple syrup		
Molasses		
Powdered sugar*		
White sugar*		

*Available in #10 cans (approximately 1 gallon)

Amount Needed for 3 Months for Family (multiply individual amount by number of family members)	Amount Needed for 6 Months for Family (multiply 3-month amount by 2)	Amount Needed for 1 Year for Family (multiply 6-month amount by 2)

(continues)

Inventory-Planning Chart

Basic Ingredients for Baking		
Item	Amount on Hand	Amount Needed for 3 Months for Individual
Fats		
Butter powder*		
Margarine powder*		
Olive or vegetable oil		
Shortening		
Shortening powder*		
Basic Spices and Flavorings		
Baking cocoa		
Chili powder		
Cinnamon		
Garlic powder		
Garlic salt		
Minced onion		
Nutmeg		
Onion powder		
Onion salt		
Pepper		
Powdered lemon		
Salt		
Vanilla		

*Available in #10 cans (approximately 1 gallon)

Amount Needed for 3 Months for Family (multiply individual amount by number of family members)	Amount Needed for 6 Months for Family (multiply 3-month amount by 2)	Amount Needed for 1 Year for Family (multiply 6-month amount by 2)

(continues)

Inventory-Planning Chart

Soups, Sauces, and Spice Mixes		
Item	Amount on Hand	Amount Needed for 3 Months for Individual
Canned Soups		
Bean and bacon		
Celery		
Chicken noodle		
Clam chowder		
Consommé		
Cream of chicken		
Cream of mushroom		
Potato		
Vegetable		
Vegetable beef		
Dehydrated Soups		
ABC soup mix*		
Corn		
Cream soup base*		
Mushroom		
Onion		
Split pea		

*Available in #10 cans (approximately 1 gallon)

Amount Needed for 3 Months for Family (multiply individual amount by number of family members)	Amount Needed for 6 Months for Family (multiply 3-month amount by 2)	Amount Needed for 1 Year for Family (multiply 6-month amount by 2)

(continues)

Inventory-Planning Chart

Soups, Sauces, and Spice Mixes		
Item	Amount on Hand	Amount Needed for 3 Months for Individual
Vegetable stew blend*		
Sauces and Spice Mixes		
Beef bouillon*		
Cheese blend*		
Chicken bouillon*		
Chili seasoning		
Gravy mixes		
Spaghetti seasoning		
Taco seasoning		
Tomato powder*		
Staples		
Cereals		
6-grain cereal*		
9-grain cereal*		
Cereals*		
Cream of wheat*		
Farina*		

*Available in #10 cans (approximately 1 gallon)

Amount Needed for 3 Months for Family (multiply individual amount by number of family members)	Amount Needed for 6 Months for Family (multiply 3-month amount by 2)	Amount Needed for 1 Year for Family (multiply 6-month amount by 2)
Staples		

(continues)

Inventory-Planning Chart

Staples		
Item	Amount on Hand	Amount Needed for 3 Months for Individual
Granola*		
Millet*		
Oatmeal* (see listing under "Basic Baking")		
Rice		
White rice*		
Grains		
Amaranth		
Barley*		
Corn meal*		
Kamut		
Oat groats, whole*		
Oats, instant*		
Pancake mix*		
Quinoa		
Rye*		
Spelt		

*Available in #10 cans (approximately 1 gallon)

Amount Needed for 3 Months for Family (multiply individual amount by number of family members)	Amount Needed for 6 Months for Family (multiply 3-month amount by 2)	Amount Needed for 1 Year for Family (multiply 6-month amount by 2)

(continues)

Inventory-Planning Chart

Staples		
Item	Amount on Hand	Amount Needed for 3 Months for Individual
Triticale		
Wheat, red*		
Wheat, white*		
White flour* (see listing under "Basic Baking")		
Whole corn*		
Legumes		
Black turtle beans*		
Kidney beans*		
Lentils*		
Lima beans, baby*		
Lima beans, large*		
Mung beans*		
Pink beans*		
Pinto beans*		
Small red beans*		
Small white navy beans*		
Soy beans*		
Split peas*		
Whole peas*		
Yellow peas*		

*Available in #10 cans (approximately 1 gallon)

Amount Needed for 3 Months for Family (multiply individual amount by number of family members)	Amount Needed for 6 Months for Family (multiply 3-month amount by 2)	Amount Needed for 1 Year for Family (multiply 6-month amount by 2)

(continues)

Inventory-Planning Chart

Item	Amount on Hand	Amount Needed for 3 Months for Individual
Staples		
Pasta		
Egg noodles*		
Fettuccini		
Lasagna		
Linguini		
Macaroni, elbow*		
Macaroni, shells*		
Spaghetti*		
Protein Foods and Dried Dairy		
Commercial and Home-Canned Fish and Meats		
Beef and rice		
Beef dices		
Beef steak		
Beef stew		
Beef stroganoff		
Chicken		
Chicken chop suey		
Chicken dices		
Chicken stew		

*Available in #10 cans (approximately 1 gallon)

Amount Needed for 3 Months for Family (multiply individual amount by number of family members)	Amount Needed for 6 Months for Family (multiply 3-month amount by 2)	Amount Needed for 1 Year for Family (multiply 6-month amount by 2)
Protein Foods and Dried Dairy		

(continues)

Inventory-Planning Chart

Protein Foods and Dried Dairy		
Item	Amount on Hand	Amount Needed for 3 Months for Individual
Chili macaroni with beef		
Clams		
Corned beef		
Deer		
Elk		
Ham		
Ham dices		
Jerky		
Kipper snacks		
Luncheon meats		
Pork		
Rabbit		
Roast beef		
Salmon		
Sausage patties		
Shrimp		
Spam		
Tuna		
Wild game		
Textured Vegetable Protein (TVP)		
Bacon bits TVP*		
Barbecue TVP*		

*Available in #10 cans (approximately 1 gallon)

Amount Needed for 3 Months for Family (multiply individual amount by number of family members)	Amount Needed for 6 Months for Family (multiply 3-month amount by 2)	Amount Needed for 1 Year for Family (multiply 6-month amount by 2)

(continues)

Inventory-Planning Chart

Protein Foods and Dried Dairy		
Item	Amount on Hand	Amount Needed for 3 Months for Individual
Beef chunks TVP*		
Chicken TVP*		
Ham TVP*		
Pepperoni TVP*		
Plain TVP*		
Pork TVP*		
Sausage TVP*		
Sloppy Joe TVP*		
Taco TVP*		
Peanut Butter		
Dry peanut butter powder*		
Regular peanut butter		
Dehydrated Eggs		
Egg mix*		
Egg whites*		
Whole eggs* (see listing under "Basic Baking")		
Dried Dairy		
Butter powder*		
Buttermilk powder* (see listing under "Basic Baking")		

*Available in #10 cans (approximately 1 gallon)

Amount Needed for 3 Months for Family (multiply individual amount by number of family members)	Amount Needed for 6 Months for Family (multiply 3-month amount by 2)	Amount Needed for 1 Year for Family (multiply 6-month amount by 2)

(continues)

Inventory-Planning Chart

Protein Foods and Dried Dairy		
Item	Amount on Hand	Amount Needed for 3 Months for Individual
Chocolate milk powder*		
Dried cheese blend*		
Instant nonfat powdered milk* (see listing under "Basic Baking")		
Regular nonfat powdered milk* (see listing under "Basic Baking")		
Sour cream powder*		

Fruits and Vegetables		
Canned Fruits		
Apple pie filling		
Applesauce		
Apricots		
Blueberries		
Cherries		
Cherry pie filling		
Fruit cocktail		
Mandarin oranges		
Nectar		
Peaches		
Pears		

*Available in #10 cans (approximately 1 gallon)

Amount Needed for 3 Months for Family (multiply individual amount by number of family members)	Amount Needed for 6 Months for Family (multiply 3-month amount by 2)	Amount Needed for 1 Year for Family (multiply 6-month amount by 2)

Fruits and Vegetables

(continues)

Inventory-Planning Chart

	Amount on Hand	for 3 Months for Individual
Fruits and Vegetables		
Item		
Pineapple		
Plums		
Dehydrated Fruits		
Apple pie filling		
Apple slices*		
Applesauce*		
Apricots		
Banana slices*		
Dates		
Figs		
Fruit blend*		
Peach-apple flakes*		
Prunes		
Raisins*		
Strawberry-apple flakes*		
Canned Vegetables		
Asparagus		
Beans, green		

*Available in #10 cans (approximately 1 gallon)

Amount Needed for 3 Months for Family (multiply individual amount by number of family members)	Amount Needed for 6 Months for Family (multiply 3-month amount by 2)	Amount Needed for 1 Year for Family (multiply 6-month amount by 2)

(continues)

Inventory-Planning Chart

Fruits and Vegetables		
Item	Amount on Hand	Amount Needed for 3 Months for Individual
Beans, kidney		
Beans, pinto		
Beets		
Carrots		
Corn, creamed		
Corn, whole		
Mushrooms		
Peas		
Peas, sweet garden		
Pork and beans		
Potatoes		
Pumpkin		
Salsa		
Squash		
Tomato juice		
Tomato sauce		
Tomatoes, stewed		
Tomatoes, whole		
Turnips		
Dehydrated Vegetables		
Bell peppers*		
Broccoli florets*		

*Available in #10 cans (approximately 1 gallon)

Amount Needed for 3 Months for Family (multiply individual amount by number of family members)	Amount Needed for 6 Months for Family (multiply 3-month amount by 2)	Amount Needed for 1 Year for Family (multiply 6-month amount by 2)

(continues)

Inventory-Planning Chart

	Fruits and Vegetables	
Item	Amount on Hand	Amount Needed for 3 Months for Individual
Cabbage*		
Carrot dices*		
Celery*		
Corn, sweet kernel*		
Green beans*		
Mushrooms*		
Onions, chopped*		
Peas, sweet*		
Potato dices*		
Potato flakes*		
Potato granules*		
Potato pearls*		
Tomato powder*		
Vegetable stew blend*		
	Fun Foods	
Dry Drink Mixes		
Hot chocolate mix*		
Lemonade*		
Orange drink mix*		

*Available in #10 cans (approximately 1 gallon)

Amount Needed for 3 Months for Family (multiply individual amount by number of family members)	Amount Needed for 6 Months for Family (multiply 3-month amount by 2)	Amount Needed for 1 Year for Family (multiply 6-month amount by 2)
Fun Foods		

(continues)

Inventory-Planning Chart

Fun Foods		
Item	Amount on Hand	Amount Needed for 3 Months for Individual
Tropical punch*		
Canned Drinks		
Apple juice		
Apricot juice		
Carrot juice		
Lemonade		
Orange juice		
Pineapple juice		
Tomato juice		
Desserts		
Dessert fillings*		
Gelatin, all flavors*		
Jams		
Jellies		
Popcorn*		
Preserves		

*Available in #10 cans (approximately 1 gallon)

Amount Needed for 3 Months for Family (multiply individual amount by number of family members)	Amount Needed for 6 Months for Family (multiply 3-month amount by 2)	Amount Needed for 1 Year for Family (multiply 6-month amount by 2)

(continues)

Inventory-Planning Chart

Fun Foods		
Item	Amount on Hand	Amount Needed for 3 Months for Individual
Puddings*		
Tapioca		
Boxed Mixes		
Bisquick		
Cake mixes		
Frosting mixes		
Hamburger Helper		
Rice-a-Roni		
Condiments		
Barbecue sauce		
Catsup		
Dill pickles		

*Available in #10 cans (approximately 1 gallon)

Amount Needed for 3 Months for Family (multiply individual amount by number of family members)	Amount Needed for 6 Months for Family (multiply 3-month amount by 2)	Amount Needed for 1 Year for Family (multiply 6-month amount by 2)

(continues)

Inventory-Planning Chart

Fun Foods		
Item	Amount on Hand	Amount Needed for 3 Months for Individual
Hot peppers		
Marinades		
Mayonnaise		
Mustard		
Olives		
Relish		
Salad dressing		
Salsa		
Sauces		
Soy sauce		
Teriyaki sauce		
Additional Spices		
Allspice, ground		
Apple pie spice		
Basil		
Bay leaves		
Celery flakes		
Cilantro flakes		
Cinnamon sticks		
Cloves, ground		
Cloves, whole		

Amount Needed for 3 Months for Family (multiply individual amount by number of family members)	Amount Needed for 6 Months for Family (multiply 3-month amount by 2)	Amount Needed for 1 Year for Family (multiply 6-month amount by 2)

(continues)

Inventory-Planning Chart

	Amount on Hand	Amount Needed for 3 Months for Individual
Fun Foods		
Item		
Cumin		
Dill seed		
Dill weed		
Ginger, ground		
Italian seasoning		
Lemon pepper		
Mustard, ground		
Oregano leaves		
Oregano, ground		
Paprika		
Parsley flakes		
Pepper, cayenne		
Pepper, white		
Peppercorns		
Pickling spice		
Poppy seeds		
Poultry seasoning		
Pumpkin pie spice		
Sage, rubbed		
Seasoning salt		
Sesame seeds		
Thyme, ground		

Amount Needed for 3 Months for Family (multiply individual amount by number of family members)	Amount Needed for 6 Months for Family (multiply 3-month amount by 2)	Amount Needed for 1 Year for Family (multiply 6-month amount by 2)

(continues)

Inventory-Planning Chart

Nonfood Items		
Item	Amount on Hand	Amount Needed for 3 Months for Individual
Paper Products		
Aluminum foil		
Garbage bags		
Napkins		
Paper bags		
Paper cups		
Paper plates		
Paper towels		
Plastic utensils		
Plastic food storage bags		
Waxed paper		
Cleansers		
Ammonia		
Bathroom cleanser		
Bleach		
Clothesline or rack		
Dish soap		
Floor cleanser		
Laundry soap		
Sink cleanser		
Washboard and tub		

Amount Needed for 3 Months for Family (multiply individual amount by number of family members)	Amount Needed for 6 Months for Family (multiply 3-month amount by 2)	Amount Needed for 1 Year for Family (multiply 6-month amount by 2)

(continues)

Inventory-Planning Chart

Nonfood Items		
Item	Amount on Hand	Amount Needed for 3 Months for Individual
Personal Hygiene		
Antibacterial soap		
Bath soap		
Bucket for toilet, with lid		
Combs		
Deodorant		
Facial moisturizer		
Feminine hygiene products		
Hair conditioner or cream rinse		
Hairbrush		
Hand lotion		
Makeup		
Personal care items		
Razor		
Razor blades		
Sanitary napkins		
Shampoo		
Toilet paper		
Toothbrush		
Toothpaste		
Towels		
Washcloths		

Amount Needed for 3 Months for Family (multiply individual amount by number of family members)	Amount Needed for 6 Months for Family (multiply 3-month amount by 2)	Amount Needed for 1 Year for Family (multiply 6-month amount by 2)

(continues)

Inventory-Planning Chart

Nonfood Items		
Item	Amount on Hand	Amount Needed for 3 Months for Individual

Replenishing Your Store

Families and individuals for whom food storage has become a way of life wisely follow this motto: "Use it or lose it."

If you wish to maintain a one-year supply of food, plan to rotate every food item so it is used up and replenished within one to three years. Rotating canned goods as well as dehydrated food will assure better quality and nutritive value. Although some items, such as dehydrated products, may keep for a long time, they too are prone to deterioration if kept for more than five to seven years. It's best to rotate them well within that time period.

When rotating food, use the oldest dated food first. Put the most recently purchased food to the back and pull from the front as you use your stored food. This is how the grocery stores do it so food doesn't get old on the shelves.

Amount Needed for 3 Months for Family (multiply individual amount by number of family members)	Amount Needed for 6 Months for Family (multiply 3-month amount by 2)	Amount Needed for 1 Year for Family (multiply 6-month amount by 2)

Prepared at Last

Once your store is stocked, you can rest easy—knowing you're prepared not only for today but for the months ahead. You will no longer need to change your dinner menu or rush to the store because you're missing an ingredient. You will have fewer worries when personal hardship strikes. You will be self-sufficient during times of crisis or disaster. You will experience peace of mind, knowing you have done all you can to be prepared for whatever your future may hold. For all your efforts, you will be rewarded with provident living.

CHAPTER 8

Recipes Using
Stored Foods

A s you read about storing enough food to sustain your family for a full year, you might have wondered just how you would prepare meals with less familiar items such as butter powder, dehydrated potato dices, or textured vegetable protein. Perhaps your mother and grandmothers did bake bread and can vegetables, but they probably did not pass on recipes that called for dried produce or TVP. This chapter focuses on preparation of stored foods, including dozens of recipes that call for dried ingredients and staples such as whole wheat or beans.

You can also adapt your own favorite recipes by replacing fresh ingredients with dried ingredients. There are two approaches to using dried ingredients: You can add water to reconstitute the products *before* adding them to the rest of your ingredients, or you can add dehydrated foods to the other dry ingredients in your recipe and add the water needed to reconstitute them to the wet ingredients. See table 7 for reconstituting guidelines.

TABLE 7. Product Reconstitution Chart

Food	Amount of Dried Food	Amount of Boiling Water	Yield
Apple (slices)	1 cup	1$1/2$ cups	2 cups
Applesauce	1 cup	3 cups	3 cups
Apricot (slices)	1 cup	2 cups	1$1/2$ cups
Banana chips	1 cup	1 cup	1$1/2$ cups
Beans and other legumes	1 cup	3 cups (+ 2 teaspoons salt)	4 cups
Beets	1 cup	3 cups	2$1/2$ cups
Bell peppers	1 cup	1$1/2$ cups	2 cups
Broccoli	1 cup	2 cups	1$1/2$ cups
Butter (powder)	1 cup	2 tablespoons	$3/4$ cup
Buttermilk	1 cup	1$1/2$ cups	2 cups
Cabbage	1 cup	2$1/2$ cups	2 cups
Carrots	1 cup	2 cups	2 cups
Celery	1 cup	1 cup	2 cups
Cheese sauce	1 cup	$1/3$ cup	$2/3$ cup
Corn (sweet)	1 cup	3 cups	2 cups
Dates	1 cup	1 cup	1$1/3$ cups
Eggs	2$1/2$ tablespoons	2$1/2$ tablespoons	1 egg
Fruit blend	1 cup	1$1/2$ cups	1$1/2$ cups
Gelatin	1 cup	4 cups	4 cups
Green beans	1 cup	2 cups	2 cups
Margarine powder	1 cup	2 tablespoons	$3/4$ cup
Milk, non-instant	1 cup	4 cups	4 cups

(continues)

TABLE 7. Product Reconstitution Chart

Food	Amount of Dried Food	Amount of Boiling Water	Yield
Mushrooms	1 cup	2 cups	1 1/2 cups
Onions	1 cup	1 cup	1 1/2 cups
Peach (slices)	1 cup	2 cups	2 cups
Peanut butter	1 cup	(4 tablespoons oil + 1/3 teaspoon sugar)	1/2 cup
Peas	1 cup	2 1/2 cups	2 1/2 cups
Peppers	1 cup	2 cups	1 1/2 cups
Potato (dices)	1 cup	3 cups	2 cups
Potato (granules)	1 cup	5 cups	5 cups
Shortening (powder)	1 cup	1 tablespoon (+ 1/2 teaspoon oil)	1/2 cup
Sour cream	1 cup	6 tablespoons	3/4 cup
Spinach (flakes)	1 cup	1 1/2 cups	1 cup
Tomato (powder)	1 cup	1 1/2 cups	1 3/4 cups
TVP meat substitute	1 cup	2 cups	1 pound
Wheat and grains	1 cup	2 cups (+ 1 teaspoon salt)	3 cups

By reviewing this chapter, you'll learn how dried and bulk foods can be incorporated into your family's diet, and you'll find excellent recipes you can use to provide yourself and your loved ones with delicious, nutritious meals.

Beans and Other Legumes

Beans are one of the staples of a home food storage program. Beans and other legumes (such as split peas, dry peas, lentils, and peanuts) contain B vitamins, minerals, carbohydrates, and fiber. When combined in a meal, rice and beans provide a complete protein. Beans and other legumes are also relatively inexpensive, which makes them especially practical to include in your food storage program.

Preparing Beans

The first step in preparing beans is to sort and rinse them. Remove any broken or odd-colored beans, rocks, or dirt that may be mixed in with them. Rinse well and drain off the water.

After beans have been sorted, rinsed, and drained, they must be soaked. For every 1 cup of dry beans, use 3 cups of water and 2 teaspoons of salt. There are two ways to soak beans: overnight or by "quick soaking." (To prevent fermentation, soybeans need to be refrigerated during soaking.)

Overnight Soaking. Combine water, salt, and beans in a pot. Cover with a lid and let stand overnight. In the morning, rinse and drain off the water. Add fresh water for cooking. This is the preferred method for soaking beans because the extended soaking time results in a more uniform texture. This is especially important when you plan to use whole beans in a salad.

Quick Soaking. Combine water, salt, and beans in a pot and bring to a boil. Continue to boil for 3 to 5 minutes. Remove from heat and cover. Let beans soak for 1 hour. Rinse and drain off the water. Add fresh water for cooking. Boiling the beans tends to split the skins, resulting in mushy beans. This method is fine, however, if you are making a recipe that calls for mashing the cooked beans, such as for refried beans or chili.

Cooking Beans

Cooking times vary widely for beans and other legumes, depending on the type (see table 8). There are several methods for cooking beans. Most people use a stovetop or oven, however, a microwave oven, slow cooker (Crock-Pot), or pressure cooker works just fine, too.

Microwave Oven. Combine water and beans in a microwave-safe dish. Use a container large enough to allow for the beans to expand to three times their current size. Cover with plastic wrap or a plastic lid. Follow your microwave appliance guide for instructions and cooking times.

Slow Cooker. You can presoak beans overnight in a Crock-Pot on a low setting. The next morning, drain soaking water, add fresh water and remaining recipe ingredients, and cook all day. Refer to the manufacturer's directions for cooking times and settings.

Pressure Cooker. Using a pressure cooker is fast, but the beans tend to split and become mushy. Presoaking will help with this problem. Fill one-third of the cooker with beans. Fill the remaining two-thirds with water. This will allow for expansion and foaming. You can minimize foaming by adding 1 to 2 tablespoons of oil. Refer to table 8 for cooking times.

The following recipe provides general guidelines for cooking beans on the stovetop.

Stovetop Beans

| 1 pound (or 2 cups) dry beans | 2 teaspoons salt |
| 6 cups water | |

Sort and wash beans. Soak overnight then drain. Add 6 cups fresh water with 2 teaspoons salt to soaked beans; bring to boil and gently simmer with the lid off. Add extra water if needed to make sure the beans don't burn. Cook until tender, 25 minutes to 2 hours, depending on the type of bean used (see table 8). Drain. Makes 6 to 7 cups.

Bean Flour

As beans get old, they are more difficult to cook. They don't seem to soften as well as newer beans. What you can do with old beans is grind them into flour using a hand or electric wheat grinder, grain mill, or blender. You can use a small amount of bean flour to replace the regular flour called for in any recipe, or use it to thicken gravies, soups, and sauces. You can also make a great bean dip by adding hot water to the bean flour and a little salt to taste, then stirring to the thickness desired.

Because beans in flour form are easier to digest, this is a great way to introduce them into your family's diet. Bean flour stores well in the refrigerator.

How to Can Beans

All kinds of beans can be canned. Soak dry beans of your choice overnight, or at least 12 hours before canning them. Place 3 cups soaked dry beans in each quart jar. Add hot water within 1 inch of the jar top. Add 1 teaspoon salt and place lid and ring on jar.

If you use a pressure cooker, process for 15 minutes at 15 pounds of pressure. Allow the cooker and jars to cool down gradually.

TABLE 8. Cooking Guidelines for Legumes

Legume Type	Dry Amount	Stovetop Time (with 1 teaspoon salt)	Pressure Cooker Time (15 pounds pressure)	Approximate Yield
Lentils	1 cup	1/2 hour	Do not pressure cook	1 1/2 cups
Lima	1 cup	2 hours	5 to 10 minutes	2 to 2 1/2 cups
Kidney	1 cup	2 hours	5 minutes	2 to 2 3/4 cups
Pinto	1 cup	2 hours	10 minutes	2 to 2 1/2 cups
Great northern	1 cup	1 to 1 1/2 hours	5 minutes	2 to 2 1/2 cups
Split peas	1 cup	1/2 hour	Do not pressure cook	2 1/2 cups
Black-eyed peas	1 cup	1/2 hour	Do not pressure cook	2 1/2 cups
Soybeans	1 cup	3 1/2 hours	10 minutes	2 to 2 1/2 cups
Black	3 cups	2 hours	5 minutes	2 cups
Navy	3 cups	2 hours	10 minutes	2 1/2 cups
Mung	1 cup	2 hours	5 minutes	2 to 2 1/2 cups

A Few Hints on Beans

- Dry beans should always be repackaged in glass or plastic containers or buckets. Store in a cool, dark place away from moisture.

- Beans can be stored for an indefinite period of time but are best if used within three years after harvesting. If beans are too old, they will not become tender when cooked. However, older beans can be ground into bean flour and added to soups and sauces as a thickener.

- Simmer beans slowly to insure uniform-looking beans that are not mushy. If cooked quickly, beans tend to split their skins. Pressure cooking is recommended only when it doesn't matter if the beans break apart.

- Add 1 to 2 tablespoons of oil to the cooking water to prevent foaming.

- To speed tenderizing, wait until the last 10 minutes of cooking time before adding salt.

- All acidic foods, such as tomatoes, lemon juice, and vinegar, should be added after the beans are tender. Acidic foods tend to lengthen the cooking time.

- Bean mixtures thicken and flavors blend as the beans cool down. Cooked beans should be kept in the refrigerator in a container with a tight-fitting lid. Beans can also be frozen and used later for another meal.

Refried Beans

2 cups dried large lima, great northern, or pinto beans	2 teaspoons salt
5 cups water	2 tablespoons vegetable oil

Sort and soak beans overnight. In a medium saucepan, combine drained soaked beans, 5 cups water, salt, and oil. Bring to a boil; reduce heat. Cover and simmer until beans are tender, 1 to 1½ hours. Drain beans, reserving the cooking liquid. Put the beans in a blender with ½ cup or more reserved cooking liquid. Blend on medium speed until smooth, stopping blender occasionally to scrape sides and to stir puree up from bottom. Bean mixture should circulate slowly. Add more water if needed. Makes 6 to 8 servings.

Pinto Bean Wheat Bread

2 tablespoons active dry yeast	½ cup evaporated milk (or ⅓ cup powdered milk reconstituted with ½ cup water)
½ cup warm water	
2 tablespoons honey	2 tablespoons vegetable oil
1 cup refried beans mixture made with pinto beans (prepare ahead using Refried Beans recipe, above)	1 tablespoon salt
	3 cups whole wheat flour (freshly ground)
1¼ cups reserved liquid (from Refried Beans recipe, above)	3 cups all-purpose white flour

Mix yeast, honey, and warm water together in a large bowl. Let stand for 10 minutes until bubbles form on the surface of the water. Combine bean mixture, reserved liquid, milk, oil, salt, and whole wheat flour. Beat until smooth. Add all-purpose white flour a little at a time until it forms a ball that clings together. You may not need to use all of the white flour. Knead on a floured surface until smooth and satiny (about 10 minutes). Grease all sides of the dough, place in a large bowl, and allow dough to double in bulk. Punch down and knead again. Shape into two loaves and place in greased baking pans.

Let it rise again until double. Bake at 375 degrees F for 45 minutes. Remove from pan and cool. Makes 2 loaves.

Boston Baked Beans

2 cups dry navy, red, or pinto beans
6 cups water (for presoaking)
1 (12-ounce) package cut up bacon (or 1/2 cup TVP bacon bits)
1 medium onion (or 1/4 cup dried onion reconstituted with 1/4 cup water)

3/4 cup brown sugar
3/4 cup ketchup (or 1/2 cup tomato powder reconstituted with 3/4 cup water)
1/2 teaspoon salt
1/2 teaspoon dry mustard
1 teaspoon chili powder
1/8 teaspoon pepper
1 clove garlic, minced

Sort, rinse, and presoak beans overnight in 6 cups water. Drain soaking water. In cooking pot, add 6 cups fresh water. Over low heat, simmer uncovered 1 hour. *Do not boil* or beans will burst. Drain beans, reserving the liquid. Place beans and all remaining ingredients into a baking dish. Add enough of the reserved liquid to beans to cover; stir well. Cover and bake at 300 degrees F for 3 1/2 hours. Makes 8 servings.

Basic Beans and Rice

Beans and rice make an excellent meal because you get a complete protein when you combine them.

3 cups beans, cooked
3 cups brown rice, cooked (add 2 tablespoons instant chicken bouillon to cooking water for more flavorful rice)

1/4 cup butter (or 1/4 cup butter powder reconstituted with 1 1/2 teaspoons water)
Salt and pepper to taste

Combine all ingredients. Serve hot. Makes 6 servings.

Western Style Beans and Rice

5 cups cooked red, kidney, or pinto beans, drained
3 medium onions, sliced (or 1 cup dried onion reconstituted with 1 cup water)
1 cup chopped green pepper (or 1/2 cup dried green pepper reconstituted with 1 cup water)
1 tablespoon butter or oil
3 (14 1/2-ounce) cans Italian-style stewed tomatoes
1 teaspoon salt
1 teaspoon chili powder
6 cups cooked rice

In a large cooking pot or Dutch oven, sauté onions and green pepper in butter. Add beans, tomatoes, and seasonings. Cover and simmer 30 to 40 minutes. Serve over rice. Makes 6 servings.

Hamburger and Bean Corn Bread Casserole

1 pound ground beef (or 1 cup beef-flavored TVP reconstituted with 2 cups water)
1/3 cup onion, chopped (or 1/6 cup dried onion reconstituted with 1/3 cup water)
1 tablespoon shortening
1 cup canned tomatoes
1 teaspoon Worcestershire sauce
2 teaspoons chili powder
1 cup cooked beans
Corn bread batter (see following recipe)

Brown meat and onion in shortening. Add tomatoes and seasonings. Cover and simmer for 15 minutes; add beans. Pour into greased 9- by 13-inch casserole dish and top with corn bread batter. Spread evenly. Bake at 425 degrees F for 20 minutes. Makes 6 servings.

Corn Bread Batter

2 cups dried corn (for grinding)	2 cups milk (or 1/2 cup powdered milk reconstituted with 2 cups water)
2 eggs (or 5 tablespoons dried whole egg powder reconstituted with 5 tablespoons water)	2 tablespoons sugar
	3/4 cup wheat flour (freshly ground)
	4 teaspoons baking powder

Grind corn using a wheat grinder. Beat eggs well and add milk and sugar. Mix flour and baking powder together with the cornmeal and egg mixture to form a soft batter. Add a little extra cornmeal if the batter is too thin (it should be thick enough to spread with a knife). Use in Hamburger and Bean Corn Bread Casserole recipe.

Beefy Chili Con Carne

2 tablespoons bacon drippings (or 2 tablespoons bacon bits TVP)	2 1/2 cups cooked or canned tomatoes
1 clove garlic, sliced	3 teaspoons chili powder
1/3 cup chopped onion (or 1/6 cup dried onion reconstituted with 1/3 cup water)	1/3 cup minced green pepper (or 1/6 cup dried green pepper reconstituted with 1/3 cup water)
1/2 pound (2 cups) ground beef (or 1/2 cup beef-flavored TVP reconstituted with 1 cup water)	1 bay leaf, crushed
	2 tablespoons sugar
2 1/2 cups cooked dry kidney or pinto beans	Salt and pepper

Brown garlic and onion in bacon drippings. Add meat or TVP and cook slowly for a few minutes, stirring occasionally. Add remaining ingredients and seasonings; simmer until meat is tender and flavors are blended (about 30 minutes). Makes 4 servings.

Basic Chili

1 pound hamburger (or 1 cup beef-flavored TVP reconstituted with 2 cups water)	1 teaspoon chili powder
	4 cups cooked beans
	1 (16-ounce) can tomato sauce
2 medium chopped onions (or 1/2 cup dried onion reconstituted with 1 cup water)	Salt and pepper to taste

Fry hamburger or TVP and onions together. Drain off the grease. Combine all remaining ingredients and simmer 1/2 hour or more (the longer you simmer, the better the taste). Add more tomato sauce if extra liquid is needed. Makes 4 servings.

Rice and Bean Salad with Sprouted Lentils

1/2 pound dry pinto or kidney beans	peppers reconstituted with 1/2 cup water)
1 pound fresh cooked green beans (or 2 cups dried green beans reconstituted with 4 cups water)	1/2 cup (or more) sprouted lentils
	1/2 cup oil
2 cups cooked brown rice	1/2 cup wine vinegar
1 cup diced celery (or 1/2 cup dried celery reconstituted with 1/2 cup water)	1 tablespoon honey
	1 teaspoon salt
	1 teaspoon pepper
1/2 cup diced green peppers (or 1/4 cup dried green	1 medium onion, sliced thin for garnish (optional)

Cover beans with water and soak overnight. Drain water, cover, and cook until just tender. Drain. Combine pinto or kidney beans, green beans, rice, celery, peppers, and lentil sprouts. In a separate bowl, combine oil, vinegar, honey, and seasonings. Toss all ingredients together. Garnish with sliced onion if desired. Makes 8 servings.

Three-Bean Salad, Vinaigrette Style

2 (15-ounce) cans pre-cooked three-bean salad mix	3 cups cooked rice
	1/2 cup salad oil
1 (15-ounce) can pre-cooked kidney beans, drained and rinsed	1/2 cup cider vinegar
	1/2 cup sugar
	Salt and pepper to taste
1 (16-ounce) can yellow wax beans	Lettuce leaves

Drain cans of beans, reserving liquid from 1 can. Combine beans, reserved liquid, rice, and remaining ingredients (except lettuce). Toss and chill. Serve over lettuce leaves. Makes 6 servings.

Bacon-Flavored Refried Beans

1 pound pinto beans	1/2 cup bacon drippings with crumbled bacon (or 1/4 cup bacon-flavored TVP reconstituted with 1/2 cup water)
6 cups water	
1 large onion, chopped (or 1/2 cup dried onion reconstituted with 1 cup water)	
	Salt to taste

Combine beans, water, and onion. Bring to boil, cover, and remove from heat for 2 hours (or soak overnight). Return to heat and simmer slowly until beans are tender, 1 to 1 1/2 hours. Mash beans, and add bacon and bacon drippings (or TVP). Continue blending until beans are thickened and fat is absorbed. Add salt to taste. Serve. These beans can be reheated. Makes 6 servings.

Pinto Bean Punch

3 1/2 cups strained pinto bean juice (see directions)
2 packages lime, strawberry, or your favorite flavor Jell-O
3 cups hot water
2 cups orange juice
2 cups pineapple juice
1 (2-liter) bottle 7-Up or Sprite

Mash up about 6 cups of cooked pinto beans; strain juice. Use only the juice, not the pulp. (If desired, save pulp for refried beans or other dishes.) Dissolve Jell-O in hot water. Add to pinto bean juice along with orange and pineapple juices. Chill. Just before serving, add chilled 7-Up or Sprite. (This recipe is surprisingly good!) Makes 20 cups.

(Recipe from Ruth Roberts)

Pinto Bean Spice Cake

1/2 cup shortening
1 cup sugar
2 beaten eggs (or 5 tablespoons dried whole egg powder reconstituted with 5 tablespoons water)
1 cup cooked pinto beans, mashed
2 cups all-purpose white flour
1/4 teaspoon salt
1 teaspoon baking powder
1/2 teaspoon soda
1 teaspoon cinnamon
1/2 teaspoon cloves
1/2 cup diced raw apple (or 1/4 cup dried apple reconstituted with 1/2 cup water)
1/2 cup raisins
1/2 cup nuts

Cream shortening, sugar, and eggs together. Mash beans and add to creamed mixture. Sift dry ingredients into mixture, add fruit and nuts, and mix well. Pour batter into greased loaf pan and bake 40 to 45 minutes at 350 degrees F. Makes 6 servings.

(Recipe from Ruth Roberts)

Pinto Bean Fudge

2/3 cup canned milk (or 1/3 cup powdered milk reconstituted with 2/3 cup water)	1 1/2 cups chocolate chips
	1/2 cups chopped nuts
1 2/3 cups sugar	1 cup cooked, strained beans (not runny)
1 1/2 cups diced marshmallows	1 teaspoon vanilla

Combine milk and sugar in a heavy pot. Boil 7 or 8 minutes, stirring constantly. Add remaining ingredients and stir until marshmallows dissolve. Pour into a buttered pan. Cool and cut into squares. (This recipe isn't especially practical for food storage, but is a good way to use up your beans!) Makes 15 servings.

(Recipe from Ruth Roberts)

Pinto Bean Applesauce Cake

1/2 cup butter (or 1/2 cup butter powder reconstituted with 1 tablespoon water)	1 teaspoon allspice
	1 teaspoon cinnamon
1 cup brown sugar	1 cup cooked mashed pinto beans
2 eggs (or 5 tablespoons dried whole egg powder reconstituted with 5 tablespoons water)	1 cup sweetened applesauce (or 1/3 cup dried applesauce reconstituted with 1 cup water)
1 cup warm water	1 cup raisins
2 cups all-purpose white flour	1 cup nuts
1 teaspoon soda	1 teaspoon vanilla
1 teaspoon salt	

Cream butter, brown sugar, and eggs. Add water and dry ingredients. Stir in beans, applesauce, raisins, nuts, and vanilla. Pour into 2 greased bread pans and bake at 350 degrees F for 40 to 50 minutes. This recipe is very good for freezing. Makes 2 loaves.

(Recipe from Ruth Roberts)

Breads

Whole wheat, which has been referred to as the "staff of life," is considered the most basic food in emergency storage programs. Wheat is easy to store, and will keep indefinitely when properly stored. Whole wheat flour, because it has not been processed, still contains the bran, germ, and endosperm. All the vitamins and minerals are still intact. Because whole wheat flour is a whole food, it is much better for our bodies than white flour, which is considered an "empty-calorie food" because so many nutrients, including the bran and wheat germ, have been removed during processing. Bleached white flour is, in fact, the base of most junk food.

In the milling process, whole wheat flour that has been freshly milled can be used to make fresh whole wheat breads. Cracked wheat can be used as breakfast cereal. Wheat can also be sprouted and added to bread.

Grinding Whole Wheat

To grind whole wheat, you will need a wheat grinder. I suggest you get a good quality electric wheat and grain grinder. If you use your grinder a lot, you will want it to last. I have a hand grinder (which is useful during electrical outages) as well as an electric grinder. Grind only as much grain as you need for the recipe because wheat is more nutritious when freshly ground than when stored preground. If you have extra ground flour, you can freeze it in a plastic bowl or plastic food storage bag. See Resource Guide for sources from which you can purchase wheat grinders.

The Art of Making Whole Wheat Bread

Bread baking is becoming a lost art. My grandmother made bread, but my mother didn't. I learned how to bake bread at the university where I earned a degree in home economics education. If I hadn't learned in school, I probably wouldn't have learned to make bread at all. We live in an era where young adults are not learning the basic skills that were so much a part of our grandmothers' generation. Even home economics programs in the schools are changing to more lecturing on life skills and less (if any) hands-on learning. Many of today's schools are in fact losing vocational funding and are unable to offer courses that teach skills such as bread baking, which I believe are very important.

People often think of bread making as some mysterious and complicated task that requires expensive equipment. In truth, it boils down to six simple steps:

1. Mix all ingredients together and knead.
2. Let the dough rise.
3. Punch down the dough.
4. Form loaves and put into bread pans.
5. Let the dough rise again.
6. Bake.

You'll need just a few kitchen tools to make bread:

- Measuring cups
- Measuring spoons
- Large bowl with lid or plastic wrap
- Bread pans
- Sharp knife
- Hot pads
- Oven
- Bread mixer (optional)

The following recipe is great for making wonderful homemade whole wheat bread. Grind your own fresh flour if possible!

Basic Whole Wheat Bread

4 cups lukewarm water	1/2 cup honey
2/3 cup powdered milk	2 teaspoons salt
3 heaping tablespoons shortening, melted	7 to 8 cups whole wheat flour (use more if needed)
2 tablespoons active dry yeast	

Step #1: Stir powdered milk in water until dissolved. Mix with shortening, yeast, and honey. Let the yeast mixture grow for about 10 minutes. Add the salt and half the flour and mix until it looks like batter. Let stand for 10 minutes. Slowly add the rest of the flour until you have a ball of dough that cleans the bowl and bounces back when you touch it. Knead the bread dough on a floured surface, such as a countertop or plastic cutting board, until it turns smooth. Knead by rubbing a little flour on your hands, forming the dough into a round ball, folding the ball toward you using the heels of your hands, then pushing it away with a rolling motion, then turning the dough a half turn and repeating until it is smooth and elastic (about 10 minutes). If the dough becomes sticky, sprinkle with a small amount of flour and continue kneading. Place dough in an oiled bowl so it doesn't stick to the sides.

Step #2: Put a clean towel, lid, or plastic wrap over the bowl; let dough rise until doubled.

Step #3: Punch dough down and remove all air bubbles.

Step #4: Shape into four loaves and place them in greased bread pans.

Step #5: Let dough rise again until it reaches about 1 inch above the pan.

Step #6: Place in the oven and bake at 350 degrees F until the loaves are nicely browned and the bread sounds hollow when you tap it. Baking time is approximately 40 to 60 minutes.

When bread is done, remove from pans. While loaves are still warm, brush tops with melted butter and let them cool. Makes 4 loaves.*

*This bread recipe can also be used for dinner rolls, bread sticks, cinnamon rolls, scones, and many other variations.

Dough Enhancer

I've talked with several friends who have a basement full of red winter wheat that they would like to use up. When they try to make bread with it, their bread doesn't rise well.

Dough enhancer, which you can use with whole wheat, strengthens the cell walls of the dough and makes the bread fluffier and lighter when baked. It not only helps the dough rise better, but is a natural preservative that helps the bread last longer on the shelf. Use two tablespoons of dough enhancer per recipe that calls for 8 to 10 cups of whole wheat flour. Do not use dough enhancer with white flour that has been processed.

Gluten Flour

Gluten is the protein in the wheat. Extra gluten is needed only when the wheat you are using has less than 15 percent protein. Using gluten flour will boost the protein content as well as help you make much lighter loaves of bread. You can add 1/3 cup of gluten flour to any recipe that calls for 8 to 10 cups of whole wheat flour.

Freshly Milled Flour

Freshly ground whole grain flour is rich in nutrients such as the wheat germ, endosperm, and bran. These nutrients are missing in white flour that has been processed. Always use freshly ground flour whenever possible.

Yeast and Other Cultures

Yeast is a small plant in the fungus family that is both airborne and growing in the soil. Yeast plants are activated by moisture and need some sort of sugar or starch to grow. When baker's or brewer's yeast ingests sugar or starch, it goes through a process known as fermentation that produces carbon dioxide gas and alcohol. This causes the bubbles to rise to the surface of the dough, thus doubling its size.

Bread-Making Hints

- Newer wheat makes the best bread; old wheat loses its elasticity and makes dense bread, but can be used for cracked wheat cereal.
- If you like the consistency of white bread, you can mix half white flour and half whole wheat flour to make a lighter, fluffier loaf of bread.
- My favorite type of wheat available on the market is called *white wheat* or *golden 86*. It is 100 percent whole wheat so it makes bread that is much better nutritionally than typical white bread; however, because the berry is a white color, when you grind and bake with it, the bread turns out white and very light and fluffy.
- Because atmospheric pressure decreases at higher altitudes, yeast batter and dough rise faster at greater elevations than they would at sea level. High altitudes also tend to be drier, so you generally need to decrease the flour. Add only enough

The yeast will grow best when combined with a sweetener such as sugar or honey and lukewarm water. Water that is too hot will kill yeast.

Rapid Rise Yeast

Rapid rise yeast was designed to shorten the rising time of the dough, and is often recommended for use in bread machines. This type of yeast is a little easier to use because it doesn't need to be flour to make the dough pliable. Grease your hands to make the dough easier to work with.

- When letting bread dough rise, you'll find it works best at 80 to 85 degrees F. So set the bowl containing your dough near a warm oven and let the heat help the dough rise. Or you can set the bowl in a deep pan of warm water and place it near your oven. Still another method is to run the bowl under hot water, then dry it thoroughly and grease it before placing the dough in it.

- To test the dough to see whether it has doubled in bulk, lightly press the tips of two fingers about 1/2 inch into the dough. If a dent remains, the dough has doubled.

- A loaf of bread should have an evenly rounded top with no bulge or dent. It will sound hollow when you tap on the bottom of the pan. Immediately remove bread from pans and cool on racks to prevent soggy-bottomed bread that results from sweating of the loaves.

dissolved like regular dry yeast, but can be added to the dry ingredients and then combined with the liquid. Rapid rise yeast also can withstand higher temperatures during activation, which makes killing it less likely.

Storage of Yeast

Keep yeast dry and cool. If the yeast has been stored in the freezer or refrigerator, it needs to be warmed up to room temperature before it is used. Be careful to avoid measuring yeast with a wet spoon because moisture will activate the yeast in the container.

The average shelf life of yeast is one year. To lengthen its shelf life, you can freeze yeast in an airtight container or keep it cool by storing it in the refrigerator. The yeast spores start to die after the expiration date, which is stamped on every package. I have used yeast that has passed its expiration date and had good results; however, I recommend you first test the yeast in a small amount of water to be sure it is still active. Mix 1 teaspoon of yeast with 2 teaspoons of lukewarm water in a bowl. Wait a few minutes; then if you see bubbles forming on top of the water, your yeast is still active. Adding sweetener to the yeast water will feed the yeast and help it grow.

Sourdough Starter

Sourdough starters have been used for centuries. Neighbors and friends would pass "starts" around and keep them going for years. It's best to grow sourdough in a crock or a glass container. Never use a metal container to store your sourdough starter, and don't leave a metal spoon in it. The yeast produces carbon dioxide and alcohol that will corrode the metal and contaminate the starter.

Sourdough Starter

Mother Starter	Sourdough Feeder
2 cups white all-purpose flour	1 cup white all-purpose flour
2 cups warm water	1 cup milk (or 1 cup water
1 package (or 1 tablespoon)	and 1/3 cup powdered milk)
active dry yeast	1/4 cup sugar

Combine the first three ingredients and store in a large plastic container or a crock. Let mixture sit for at least 24 hours in a warm place.

Keep a lid on it or otherwise cover it. This mixture, called the "mother starter," will be "fed" with Sourdough Feeder on the second day, and thereafter each time you use some of it. To "feed," add the last three ingredients to the mother starter and let stand for another 24 hours, then it's ready to use.

Each time you use some of the starter, always save at least 1/2 cup to mix with your next feeder batch. Let your mixture of starter and feeder stand in a warm place for another 24-hour period before using or refrigerating.

Potato Water Sourdough Starter (Airborne Yeast Method)

2 cups unbleached white flour	1 tablespoon sugar or honey
2 cups cool potato water	

Mix flour, potato water (what is left over after you boil potatoes), and sugar or honey together until mixture is spongy. Let it sit for 24 hours in a plastic or glass container. Starter is ready when the mixture bubbles, smells yeasty, and has doubled in size.

If the mixture molds or smells bad, then it has not captured the wild yeast from the air; throw it away and start over.

The sourdough gets better after a few days in the refrigerator. As you use it and feed it, it will taste even better. Sourdough also can be frozen and thawed out before using.

Converting Recipes to Sourdough

Any recipe that calls for yeast can be converted to sourdough by adding 1/2 cup of sourdough starter in place of one tablespoon of yeast and decreasing the liquid by 1/2 cup and the flour by 1/2 cup in the recipe. The secret is to keep the consistency and moisture about the same. Mix the starter into the liquid called for in the recipe, add some of the flour, and stir. This conversion will work for any recipe that calls for 6 or more cups of flour.

When adding sourdough, first make the "sponge" by combining the starter, the water, and the flour from the recipe. Let this sponge sit in a bowl at room temperature for at least 4 hours. If you want a more potent sour flavor, let it stand overnight (the longer it sits, the more sour the flavor). Next combine the remaining ingredients and proceed with the recipe. Then knead, rise, and shape the dough as usual.

If you are making batter bread or cakes, it's a good idea to let your batter sit in the pan for a while so it has time to bubble up and activate the sourdough.

Sourdough Whole Wheat Pancakes

1 cup sourdough starter
2 tablespoons honey
2 cups warm milk (or 1/2 cup powdered milk reconstituted with 2 cups warm water)
2 beaten eggs (or 5 table-spoons dried whole egg powder reconstituted with 5 tablespoons water)

2 to 2 1/2 cups whole wheat flour (freshly ground)
1/2 teaspoon salt
1/4 cup melted butter or olive oil
1/2 teaspoon baking soda

Mix sourdough starter, honey, warm milk, and beaten eggs in a bowl. In another bowl, mix flour and salt. Add dry ingredients to wet ingredients. Because this is a sourdough recipe, the mixture will need to stand in the refrigerator overnight to activate the sourdough. The next morning, add 1/4 cup melted butter or olive oil and 1/2 teaspoon baking soda. Mix batter well and fry pancakes on a lightly oiled skillet or frying pan. Makes ten 5-inch pancakes.

Basic Sourdough Biscuits

1 1/2 cups all-purpose white flour	1 1/2 teaspoons baking soda
2 tablespoons sugar	3 teaspoons baking powder
1 teaspoon salt	1/4 cup melted shortening
	1 1/2 cups sourdough starter

In a large bowl, mix all dry ingredients together. Make a hole in the center of the flour mixture then add melted shortening and sourdough starter. Mix well. Knead on a floured surface until dough sticks together. Roll out to about 1/2 inch thick. Using the rim of a glass or cookie cutter, cut out round biscuits. Grease a 9-by-13-inch cookie sheet and place biscuits on it, turning them to coat both sides. Let rise for at least 1/2 hour. Bake at 425 degrees F for 15 to 20 minutes. Makes 15 biscuits.

Whole Wheat Blender Pancakes

1 1/2 cups milk (or 3/8 cup powdered milk reconstituted with 1 1/2 cups water)	reconstituted with 5 tablespoons water)
1 1/2 cups whole wheat (freshly ground)	3 tablespoons melted butter (or 3 tablespoons butter powder reconstituted with a few drops water)
1 tablespoon baking powder	1/2 teaspoon salt
2 eggs (or 5 tablespoons dried whole egg powder	

If you do not have access to a wheat grinder, you can use a blender to grind the wheat for this recipe. First put the milk in the blender then add the whole wheat a little at a time through the hole in the top of the blender lid. The wheat must be ground up to the fine state. Then add the remaining ingredients until the batter is blended. Oil the griddle or skillet, pour the batter on it in about 5-inch circles. When one side is brown, flip pancakes over and brown the other side. Makes ten 5-inch pancakes.

Whole Wheat Biscuits

1/2 cup powdered milk
4 cups whole wheat flour (or
   half white flour and half
   whole wheat flour)
2 tablespoons baking powder
1 teaspoon salt

1/2 cup shortening or butter
   (or 1/2 cup butter powder
   reconstituted with 1 tablespoon water)
1 1/2 cups water

Preheat oven to 400 degrees F. Mix dry ingredients together. Add the shortening or butter and cut it in with a knife or pastry cutter until the mixture forms pea-sized balls of dough. Add water into a hole in the middle of the flour and butter mixture. Stir enough to moisten all the dry ingredients. Knead the dough on a floured surface until it sticks together. Do not overmix the dough or your biscuits won't be light and fluffy. Roll out to about 1/2 inch thick and cut with the lip of a 2-inch glass or a round cookie cutter. Bake on the top oven rack for 10 to 12 minutes or until golden brown. Makes 12 to 15 biscuits.

How to Cook Whole Wheat

When cooking wheat, the rule of thumb is to use 2 cups of water and 1/2 teaspoon salt for 1 cup of wheat. Place ingredients into saucepan, bring to a full boil, then turn heat down and simmer until the wheat is tender. Stir occasionally. Add a little more water if needed.

Note: Always wash whole wheat kernels before cooking to remove any dirt or insects that may have gotten into the wheat during storage.

Cracked Whole Wheat Cereal

1 cup freshly cracked wheat	1 tablespoon butter (or 1
3 cups water	tablespoon butter powder
1/2 teaspoon salt	reconstituted with a few
	drops water)

Combine all ingredients in a pan. Bring to a full boil and reduce the heat. Simmer 20 minutes. Serve with honey, raisins, and milk. This cereal is also delicious with chopped apples, berries, nuts such as almonds or cashews, sunflower seeds, or cinnamon. Makes 2 servings.

Whole Wheat Breakfast Cereal

2 cups whole wheat	1 teaspoon salt
4 cups water	

Mix wheat, water, and salt in a saucepan; bring to a boil. Turn stove down to low and simmer another 15 to 20 minutes, or until the wheat softens and becomes tender. Serve with honey, fruit such as berries or raisins, or nuts. Makes 4 servings.

Thermos Wheat Cereal

This recipe is great for busy people who don't have time to prepare a nutritious breakfast in the morning.

4 cups water	
1/2 cup whole wheat	

Boil 4 cups of water and pour into a thermos. Add rinsed whole wheat kernels. Screw on thermos lid and leave overnight. The next morning, drain off the water and serve the whole wheat cereal in a bowl with honey and milk. Add raisins or fruit if desired. Makes 2 servings.

Steamed Wheat

1 cup whole wheat	1/2 teaspoon salt
2 cups water	

Rinse whole wheat kernels first to remove dirt or insects. Use a steamer with water in the bottom to steam the wheat. Bring water to a boil, cover the pan with a lid, reduce heat, and steam wheat until tender, about 20 minutes. This method makes plump and fluffy wheat berries. Makes 4 (1/2-cup) servings.

Whole Wheat Flour Tortillas

6 cups whole wheat flour	reconstituted with 2 table-
1 teaspoon salt	spoons water)
1/2 cup milk (or 1/8 cup pow-	1 egg (or 2 1/2 tablespoons
dered milk reconstituted	dried whole egg powder re-
with 1/2 cup water)	constituted with 2 1/2 table-
1 tablespoon baking soda	spoons water)
1 cup shortening or cold but-	2 cups water
ter (or 1 cup butter powder	1 tablespoon vinegar

Mix flour, salt, milk, and baking soda in large bowl. Cut in shortening or butter with a pastry cutter or knife until it forms pea-sized balls. In another bowl, beat the egg slightly; mix in water and vinegar. Add wet ingredients to dry ingredients and stir until batter forms a soft dough. Knead a few times until dough is mixed well. Divide into 10 balls and roll them out thin, 8 inches across and 1/4 inch thick. Use flour to keep the dough from sticking to the countertop. Fry in ungreased pan or on griddle. Turn as tortillas brown and bubble a little. Makes 10 tortillas.

Whole Wheat Pizza

1 tablespoon (or 1 package) active dry yeast	1 tablespoon olive oil
1 cup warm water	1 teaspoon honey or 2 teaspoons sugar
4 cups whole wheat flour (freshly ground)	1 teaspoon salt

Mix yeast with 1 cup warm water. Let it activate for 10 minutes until it bubbles on the top of the water. Add remaining ingredients. Knead the dough until it is smooth. Let the dough rise for 1 hour, or until double in size. Roll dough out on a floured countertop or other surface until the desired size for your pizza. Top rolled-out pizza dough with cheese (mozzarella is best), pizza sauce (or other tomato-based sauce), vegetables (such as onions, green peppers, and olives), and meats (such as pepperoni, hamburger, ham, or bacon). If desired, substitute reconstituted vegetables and TVP in place of fresh vegetables and meat. Bake at 500 degrees F for 8 to 10 minutes. Makes one large pizza.

Whole Wheat Egg Noodles

3 eggs (or $1/2$ cup dried whole egg powder reconstituted with $1/2$ cup water)	milk reconstituted with 3 tablespoons water)
2 tablespoons butter (or 2 tablespoons butter powder reconstituted with a few drops water)	1 teaspoon salt
	Pepper to taste
	$1/4$ teaspoon baking powder
3 tablespoons milk (or 2 teaspoons powdered	2 cups whole wheat flour (freshly ground)

Mix all ingredients together except the flour. Add flour a little at a time until it forms a stiff dough. Roll out dough on a floured surface to $1/8$-inch thickness. Cut into strips approximately $1/4$- to $1/2$-inch wide and 4 inches long. Let dry for about an hour if possible. Use these noodles in your favorite chicken noodle soup or pasta dishes. Boil before serving by dropping them into the soup stock or boiling water. The noodles are done when they rise to the top of the pot. Makes $1/2$ gallon of noodles.

More Ideas for Using Wheat

- Use a Crock Pot, double boiler, or rice cooker to cook the wheat.
- Substitute wheat for rice or beans in any recipe. For example, make wheat chili or baked wheat instead of baked beans.
- Use wheat as a breakfast cereal. Add honey, nuts, fruit such as raisins or dates, and milk or cream.
- Cook the wheat as you would rice, adding bouillon to flavor the water. Sauté onions, celery, mushrooms, and other vegetables of your choice to make a wheat pilaf.
- Mix any gravy or cream sauce with wheat and bake in a casserole dish with cheese on top.

Basic White Bread Rolls

1 3/4 cups milk (or 3/8 cup powdered milk reconstituted with 1 3/4 cups water)	1 tablespoon (or 1 package) active dry yeast
1/4 cup sugar	1 beaten egg (or 2 1/2 tablespoons dried whole egg powder reconstituted with 2 1/2 tablespoons water)
1/4 cup shortening or oil	
1 teaspoon salt	
1 cup all-purpose white flour	6 to 7 cups all-purpose white flour

Place milk, sugar, shortening, and salt in a large bowl; stir mixture. In small bowl, mix 1 cup white flour with yeast and add to mixture in large bowl. Stir until the yeast and all the ingredients are completely dissolved. Add the beaten egg and enough flour to create a moderately stiff dough. Knead dough for at least 10 minutes on a floured surface. Place dough in a large greased bowl and let rise until double in bulk.

- Substitute wheat for rice in any fried rice dish, mixing it with chopped ham and sautéed vegetables.
- Extend hamburger for tacos by adding cooked wheat berries. Use half beef and half wheat.
- Grind cooked wheat and mix it with uncooked salmon, tuna, hamburger, roast beef, Spam, and spices. Form the mixture into patties; fry patties as you would hamburgers.
- Sprout wheat and use it when the sprout is about half the size of the wheat kernel. Once wheat sprouts, it becomes much more nutritious.

Punch down and let dough rise again until double. Shape into rolls or crescents. Place on a greased cookie sheet 1 inch apart and let rise one more time. Bake at 375 degrees F until golden brown, about 25 minutes. Remove rolls from the cookie sheet to cool. You can use this recipe for loaves of white bread also. Makes 2 loaves or 24 rolls.

(Recipe from Debbie Hampton)

100% Whole Wheat Bread or Rolls

1 3/4 cups lukewarm water
1/4 cup honey
1/2 cup shortening
1 teaspoon salt
1 package active dry yeast
1/4 cup warm water

1 beaten egg (or 2 1/2 tablespoons dried whole egg powder reconstituted with 2 1/2 tablespoons water)
6 to 7 cups whole wheat flour

Mix lukewarm water, honey, shortening, and salt together. In a separate bowl, dissolve yeast in 1/4 cup warm water. Add 1 cup flour; stir until dissolved. Add the egg, then gradually add flour, 1 cup at a time, until moderately stiff dough is formed. Use the amount of flour you need to form dough that isn't sticky and pulls away from the bowl. Knead this dough until it is smooth and elastic. Place dough in a large greased bowl and allow to rise until double in size. Punch down and form the dough into 2 loaves (if making bread) and place in greased bread pans. Bake at 375 degrees F until golden brown (about 35 minutes).

If you are making rolls, form 3/4-inch balls, roll them in melted butter, and place 3 balls in each muffin tin cup to form clover-shape rolls. Bake at 375 degrees F until golden brown (about 25 minutes). Makes 2 loaves of bread or 24 cloverleaf rolls.

(Recipe from Debbie Hampton)

Half White, Half Whole Wheat Bread

1³/4 cups warm water	1 package active dry yeast
1/4 cup honey or brown sugar	3¹/2 cups whole wheat flour
3 tablespoons shortening or	(freshly ground)
oil	3¹/2 cups all-purpose white
1 teaspoon salt	flour

Mix warm water, honey or brown sugar, shortening or oil, and salt together in a large bowl until the shortening melts. Add 1 cup all-purpose white flour and dry yeast; mix thoroughly. Next add 1 cup wheat flour and continue mixing. Continue adding 1 cup all-purpose white flour and 1 cup whole wheat flour alternately until the dough form a ball. Knead dough on a floured surface for at least 10 minutes or until smooth and elastic. Keep surface floured as you knead. Grease a large bowl, place dough in it, and let rise until double. Punch dough down, cover, and let rise again until double in bulk. Shape into two loaves and place each in a greased bread pan. Let loaves rise to about 1 inch over the pan. Bake in a preheated oven at 375 degrees F until golden brown (about 35 minutes). Remove bread from pans to cool (to prevent soggy bread). Cut and serve when cool. Makes 2 loaves.

(Recipe from Debbie Hampton)

Quick Breads

Quick breads can be made more quickly than yeast breads because they are made from batter rather than dough. This type of bread, which is often more like cake than bread, include muffins, banana nut bread, zucchini bread, coffee cakes, apple spice bread, and corn bread. Quick breads are very easy to make and can be made with reconstituted dehydrated foods.

Basic Muffins

2 1/2 tablespoons dried whole egg powder (or 1 egg)	3/4 teaspoon salt
	3 tablespoons sugar
1 3/4 cups all-purpose white flour	1/4 cup melted shortening
	1 2/3 cups water
2 1/2 teaspoons baking powder	3/4 cup powdered milk

Sift together the dried egg, flour, baking powder, salt, and sugar. In a separate bowl, combine the shortening, water, and powdered milk. Add to dry ingredients, stirring only enough to moisten. Fill greased muffin pans 2/3 full with the mixture. Bake at 375 degrees F for 20 minutes. Makes 12 large or 14 medium muffins.

Variations:

Add blueberries, chopped nuts, bananas, carrots, apple dices, raisins, or granola to muffin batter.

Whole Wheat Zucchini Bread

3 eggs (or 1/2 cup dried whole egg powder reconstituted with 1/2 cup water)	1 teaspoon salt
	1 teaspoon vanilla
	3 cups whole wheat flour (freshly ground)
1 cup vegetable oil	
1 1/2 cups sugar	2 cups grated zucchini
1 teaspoon baking soda	1 cup chopped walnuts

Preheat oven to 350 degrees F. Mix eggs, oil, sugar, baking soda, salt, and vanilla in a bowl until creamy. Mix in 1 cup whole wheat flour and 1 cup grated zucchini, then add remaining flour and zucchini. Mix well. Add nuts. Pour into two greased bread pans and bake for approximately 50 minutes. To test for doneness, stick a toothpick in the center; if it comes out clean, bread is ready. Makes 2 loaves.

Corn Bread

2 cups cornmeal (freshly ground, if possible)	1 3/4 cups water
	1 cup buttermilk powder
1/2 teaspoon baking soda	1/3 cup dried whole egg powder (or 2 eggs)
2 teaspoons baking powder	
1 teaspoon salt	2 tablespoons oil

Sift together cornmeal, baking soda, baking powder, and salt. Combine water, dry buttermilk, dry egg, and oil; blend well. Add to dry ingredients, stirring just enough to moisten. Pour into a greased 8- by 8-inch pan. Bake at 425 degrees F for 30 minutes. Makes 4 servings.

Dried Eggs

Dried egg powder is an excellent substitute for fresh eggs. It is high in protein, easy to store, easy to use, and works as well as fresh eggs in most recipes. You can buy either *dried whole egg powder,* which is 100 percent egg product or *dried egg mix,* which contains dried whole egg, powdered milk, and butter powder. Dried egg mix is more of a scrambled egg mixture that makes a fluffier omelet or scrambled egg.

How to Store Dried Eggs

Store unopened bags or cans of dried egg powder in a cool, dry place off the floor. Once you open containers, store dried egg products in the refrigerator (32 to 40 degrees F). They should have a tight-fitting lid or be stored in a sealed plastic food bag. You can store good-quality eggs up to one year after opening them when you maintain proper conditions.

Shelf Life of Dried Eggs

The recommended shelf life of dried eggs (unopened) is three to five years. Although it's better to rotate them more often, you can increase the length of storage time by keeping them below 40 degrees F and in a can sealed with nitrogen rather than in an oxygen environment.

Reconstituting Dried Eggs

You can reconstitute dried eggs by using either of two methods:

Method #1. Measure dried egg powder, level off the top of measuring cup with a knife. Put warm water in a bowl, sprinkle or sift the powder over the water, and whip until smooth. Reconstitute only the amount needed. Throw away any leftovers.

Method #2. Sift and measure dried egg powder, then combine with other dry ingredients in recipe. Add the water needed to reconstitute the dried egg powder to other liquids in recipe.

TABLE 9. Dried Egg Reconstitution Chart

Amount Product	Warm Water	Yields
Dried Whole Egg Powder		
2 1/2 tablespoons	2 1/2 tablespoons	1 egg
5 tablespoons	5 tablespoons	2 eggs
1/2 cup	1/2 cup	3 eggs
2/3 cup	2/3 cup	4 eggs
3/4 cup	3/4 cup	5 eggs
1 cup	1 cup	6 eggs
Dried Egg Mix		
2 tablespoons	3 tablespoons	1 egg
4 tablespoons	6 tablespoons	2 eggs
6 tablespoons	9 tablespoons	3 eggs
1/2 cup	3/4 cup	4 eggs
5/8 cup	7/8 cup	5 eggs
3/4 cup	1 1/8 cup	6 eggs

If you wish to substitute dried for fresh eggs in a recipe, use table 9 to determine how much water and either dried whole egg powder or dried egg mix you need.

Converting Recipes Using Dried Eggs

Any recipe calling for dried eggs can be converted back to whole fresh eggs by substituting the appropriate number of fresh eggs for amounts of dried egg powder and water called for in table 9.

Scrambled Eggs Mix

3/4 cup dried egg mix	1 tablespoon butter
1 1/8 cups warm water	

Sprinkle dried egg over water and blend well. Melt butter in a frying pan. Add egg mixture and stir until eggs are firm. Makes 6 one-egg servings.

Scrambled Whole Eggs

1 cup dried whole egg powder	2 tablespoons powdered milk
1 1/2 cups water	1 tablespoon butter
1/2 tablespoon salt	

Sprinkle dried egg over the water and beat to blend. Add salt and powdered milk; mix. Melt butter in a frying pan. Cook eggs over low heat, stirring continuously until they reach desired consistency. For flavor, add TVP bacon bits. Makes 6 one-egg servings.

Baked Scrambled Eggs

1 cup sifted dried whole egg powder	3 tablespoons powdered milk
1 cup water	2/3 cup water
1/2 teaspoon salt	2 tablespoons butter

Sprinkle dried whole egg powder over 1 cup water, stir to moisten, and beat until smooth. Stir in salt, powdered milk, and 2/3 cup water. Mix well. Place butter in an 8- by 8-inch baking pan. Pour mixture into pan. Bake at 350 degrees F. After 15 minutes, stir the egg mixture. Bake 5 minutes longer. Makes 6 one-egg servings.

Variations:

• Add chopped green chilies and 1/2 teaspoon dried cheese powder stirred into 1/4 teaspoon water. Sprinkle cheese and chilies over egg mixture just before it sets.

- Add ½ teaspoon TVP bacon bits before egg mixture is set.
- Add reconstituted bell peppers and ½ teaspoon dried minced onions. Cook in soufflé or baking pan in a 350-degree F oven until a toothpick inserted into the center of egg mixture comes out clean.
- Add chicken chunks to egg mixture just before cooking.
- Place ⅔ cup water in a saucepan; add ¼ cup dried tomatoes, ½ teaspoon dried green bell pepper, ½ teaspoon minced onion. Cook until tender. Add ½ teaspoon sugar and ¼ teaspoon salt to season. Serve over scrambled eggs.

Crispy Strawberry Waffles

3 tablespoons dried egg whites (or 2 fresh egg whites)	1 tablespoon baking powder
	1 teaspoon salt
	2 tablespoons sugar
6 tablespoons warm water	½ cup oil
2 cups all-purpose white flour	1 cup plus 2 tablespoons water
3 teaspoons dried egg yolk (or 2 fresh egg yolks)	2 cups sliced strawberries
¼ cup powdered milk	1 cup whipped cream

ᵃx dried egg white with 6 tablespoons warm water (or use 2 fresh egg
ᵃs and no water). Beat until stiff. In a separate bowl, sift dry ingredi-
ᵃether; add oil and 1 cup plus 2 tablespoons of water. Mix until
ᵃtened. Fold in beaten egg whites. Bake on hot waffle iron. Top
ᵃrawberries and whipped cream. Makes 6 servings.

ᵃd whole

	⅛ teaspoon cinnamon (optional)
	⅛ teaspoon sugar (optional)
	6 slices of bread

221

Combine dried whole egg powder with powdered milk and mix with water. Add salt and, if desired, a bit of cinnamon and sugar to the egg mixture. Dip each slice of bread (stale bread makes the best French toast) in egg mixture and fry on each side. Top with syrup, jam, or fresh fruit. Makes 6 servings.

Fluffy Buttermilk Pancakes

2 cups white or wheat flour (freshly ground)	1 teaspoon baking soda
$1/3$ cup dried buttermilk	$1/2$ teaspoon salt
$1/4$ cup powdered milk	2 tablespoons baking powder
6 tablespoons dried whole egg powder	$2^{1}/2$ cups warm water
	$1/3$ cup oil
	3 tablespoons honey or sugar

Mix dry ingredients well. Add water, oil, and honey or sugar. Mix well and pour 5-inch circles on a hot griddle. When pancakes are lightly browned on one side, flip over and cook on the other. Serve with desired topping. Makes twelve 5-inch pancakes.

Whole Wheat Pancakes

2 cups whole wheat flour	6 tablespoons powdered milk
2 teaspoons baking powder	$1/2$ teaspoon salt
4 tablespoons sugar	2 cups plus 5 tablespoons water
5 tablespoons dried whole egg powder	4 tablespoons oil

Sift dry ingredients. Add water and oil; stir until moist. Cook o' griddle or pan at medium heat. Serve with your favorite topp Makes twelve 5-inch pancakes.

German Pancakes

3 cups warm water	1/2 teaspoon salt
1 cup dried whole egg powder	1 cup all-purpose white flour
3 tablespoons powdered milk	1/2 cup butter

Mix water, dried whole egg powder, powdered milk, and salt in a blender until fluffy. Mix in flour a little at a time; beat until well blended. Melt butter in 9- by 13-inch pan at 425 degrees F. When butter is bubbly, pour batter into pan and return to the oven immediately. Bake 25 minutes. Serve with fruit, jam, syrup, powdered sugar, peanut butter, or whipped topping. Makes 9 servings.

Chicken and Dumplings

1 whole chicken	1 1/4 teaspoons baking powder
Dumplings	1/2 teaspoon salt
1/3 cup sifted dried whole egg powder	1 1/2 tablespoons margarine or butter
1 cup all-purpose white flour	1/2 cup water
2 tablespoons powdered milk	

ˉook chicken in a pot of water. Save broth and debone chicken. For ˙nplings: Sift dry ingredients together. Cut in margarine or butter ˙mixture is the consistency of cornmeal. Add water to the flour and mix just to moisten the dry ingredients. Drop by table- ˙into boiling chicken broth. Cover and cook 12 minutes. Do ˙over during the cooking period. Add pieces of deboned ˙ to the broth to make a thick soup. Makes 6 servings.

223

Dried Fruits

Applesauce Cinnamon Cake

1/2 cup dried applesauce	3/4 cup shortening powder
1 teaspoon cinnamon	1 1/4 cups water
1 cup sugar	3/4 teaspoon baking soda
2 cups all-purpose white flour	1 cup raisins

Mix all ingredients together until smooth. Pour the batter into a greased and floured 9- by 13-inch cake pan. Bake at 350 degrees F for 35 minutes. Makes 1 cake, approximately 15 servings.

Apple Pie Filling

2 cups dried apple slices	1/2 teaspoon cinnamon
2 1/2 cups water	1/4 teaspoon nutmeg
2/3 cup sugar	2 teaspoons dried lemon
2 tablespoons cornstarch	powder or juice
1/4 teaspoon salt	

Mix all ingredients together in a saucepan. Bring mixture to boil, stirring occasionally. For a pie, put mixture in 9-inch pie shell and bake at 450 degrees F for 40 minutes. To make filling, continue to cook until mixture thickens and apples are tender. Makes 6 servings.

Apple Crisp

Apple Pie Filling (see previous recipe)	4 tablespoons sugar
	1/2 teaspoon salt
1 teaspoon cinnamon	1/2 cup butter powder
1/2 cup quick rolled oats	1/2 cup all-purpose white flour

Pour Apple Pie Filling into 9-inch pie tin. Mix remaining ingredients in a bowl, then spread over pie filling. Bake at 375 degrees F for 25 minutes. Makes 6 servings.

Applesauce

1 cup dried applesauce	1/2 teaspoon cinnamon
1 cup water	(optional)
1 teaspoon sugar	

Mix all the ingredients together and let stand for 10 minutes. Use mixture in any recipe calling for applesauce. Makes 4 servings.

Applesauce Spice Bread

3/4 cup all-purpose white flour	3/4 cup dried applesauce reconstituted with 3/4 cup water
3/4 cup whole wheat flour	
1 teaspoon cinnamon	
1/2 teaspoon nutmeg	1 cup dried apples, reconstituted with 2 cups water
1/2 teaspoon mace	
1 teaspoon allspice	2 eggs (or 5 tablespoons dried whole egg powder reconstituted with 5 tablespoons water)
1 teaspoon baking soda	
1 teaspoon baking powder	
1/2 teaspoon salt	
2/3 cup butter (or 2/3 cup butter powder reconstituted with 1 1/2 tablespoons water)	1 cup rolled oats
	3/4 cup chopped walnuts
1/4 cup brown sugar	1 cup raisins

In a large bowl, combine flours, spices, baking powder, baking soda, and salt. In another bowl, combine butter and sugar until creamy. Add applesauce, apple, and eggs. Combine the two mixtures, stirring well. Add oats, walnuts, and raisins, and mix well again. Grease a 9-by 13-inch cake pan and pour the batter into the pan. Bake at 350 degrees F until it springs up when lightly touched in the middle, about 30 to 35 minutes. Cool and serve. Makes 12 servings.

RECIPES USING STORED FOODS

Banana Bread

1 cup dried banana chips	1/4 cup dried whole egg
1 cup water	powder
1/2 cup dried shortening	1 1/2 teaspoons baking powder
powder	1/2 teaspoon salt
1 cup sugar	1 teaspoon cinnamon
2 cups all-purpose white flour	

Reconstitute the banana chips by soaking them in the 1 cup water. Mix with all remaining ingredients. If the batter is stiff, add a little more water. Pour the batter into a greased 9- by 13-inch cake pan and bake at 350 degrees F for 1 hour and 20 minutes, or until the cake springs back when touched in the center. Cool and serve with butter. Makes 12 servings.

Reconstituted Fruit Cocktail

2 3/4 cups water	1 cup dried fruit cocktail

Bring ingredients to a boil and cover for 10 minutes. Use in any recipe that calls for fruit cocktail. Makes 4 (1-cup) servings.

Gelatin Fruit Salad

1 cup strawberry-flavored	1 cup reconstituted fruit
gelatin	cocktail
4 cups water	

Pour gelatin into bowl. In a saucepan, bring half the water (2 cups) to a rolling boil. Pour boiling water over gelatin and stir until dissolved. Add remaining 2 cups of water and reconstituted fruit cocktail. Chill until thickened. Add whipped topping if desired. Makes 6 servings.

Dried Potatoes

Dried potatoes are an excellent replacement for fresh potatoes, as well as easy to store and prepare. The following recipes represent just a few of the many ways dried potatoes can be prepared.

Mashed Potatoes

8 cups hot water	powder reconstituted with
3 cups potato flakes	1 teaspoon water)
4 tablespoons butter	
(or 4 tablespoons butter	

Boil water. Add potato flakes and butter; whip until mixture fluffs up. Let stand for a few minutes. Add salt and pepper to taste. Makes 6 cups.

Potato Patties

3 1/2 cups mashed potatoes	1/4 teaspoon pepper
1/4 cup butter (or 1/4 cup but-	5 tablespoons dried whole
ter powder reconstituted	egg powder
with 1 1/2 teaspoons water)	5 tablespoons water
1 teaspoon salt	

In a large bowl, beat potatoes, butter, salt, and pepper at low speed with an electric beater, until light and fluffy. Mix dried whole egg powder and water together. Add to potato mixture and beat at medium speed until well blended. To make the patties, use about 1/4 cup of the mixture to form each patty, then fry in lightly greased pan over medium-high heat until browned on both sides, about 2 to 3 minutes. Makes about 15 patties.

Dried Hash Brown Potatoes

1 1/2 cups dried hash brown potatoes	8 cups hot water

To reconstitute hash brown potatoes, add hot water and let stand for 20 minutes until the potatoes are tender. Drain the water and fry the hash browns on a well-greased griddle until golden brown on one side. Flip them over and brown the other side. Makes 6 (1/2-cup) servings.

Potato Slices and Dices

1 cup sliced or diced dried potato	3 cups hot water

To reconstitute, add hot water to dried potatoes and let stand until potatoes are tender, about 30 minutes. Use the slices or dices for chowders, soups, casseroles, main dishes, or any other recipe calling for potatoes. Makes 3 cups.

Peanut Butter (from Peanut Butter Powder)

1 cup peanut butter powder 4 tablespoons vegetable oil	Pinch of sugar

Combine all ingredients in a bowl. Slowly blend until you reach the desired consistency of peanut butter. Peanut butter powder can be reconstituted and used in any recipe calling for regular peanut butter. Makes 1 cup.

Powdered Milk and Dairy

There are two types of powdered milk:

Instant nonfat powdered milk is made by a process that results in larger particles or flakes than regular powdered milk. It is easy to mix with a spoon or blender because it dissolves easily in water. Chill overnight for best flavor for drinking.

Non-instant or regular powdered milk is more difficult to mix than instant milk. Mix with hot water. Blend in blender or with a wire whip, then refrigerate until well chilled before drinking.

Reconstituted powdered milk can be a substitute in any recipe that calls for milk. Not only is it less expensive than fresh or canned milk, but in most cases it contains the same nutrients except for fat; therefore, it has less cholesterol and fewer calories.

Any recipe calling for fluid milk can be converted to powdered milk by using the equivalents listed in table 10. Simply replace the amount of milk required with an equal amount of water, then add the appropriate amount of powdered milk to the other dry ingredients in a recipe.

How to Blend Powdered Milk

1. Fill blender half full with water.

2. Turn blender on low and add powdered milk. (A hand mixer or wire whip can be used also.) Make sure the blender is going before you add milk powder to water so milk won't become lumpy.

3. To avoid foam on top of the milk, mix only long enough to blend.

TABLE 10. Powdered Milk Reconstitution Chart

Amount of of Water	Instant Powdered Milk	Non-Instant or Regular Powdered Milk	Yield
1/4 cup	1 tablespoon	3/4 tablespoon	1/4 cup
1/3 cup	1 1/2 tablespoons	1 1/4 tablespoons	1/3 cup
1/2 cup	2 tablespoons	1 1/2 tablespoons	1/2 cup
2/3 cup	3 tablespoons	2 1/2 tablespoons	2/3 cup
1 cup	1/4 cup	3 tablespoons	1 cup
1 pint	1/2 cup	1/3 cup	1 pint
1 quart	1 cup	3/4 cup	1 quart
1/2 gallon	2 cups	1 1/2 cups	1/2 gallon
1 gallon	4 cups	3 cups	1 gallon

4. Pour into a large container. Add remaining water. Stir well. For best results, mix and chill overnight before using.

5. Store reconstituted milk in the refrigerator after mixing— just like fresh milk.

Shelf Life of Powdered Milk

You can keep powdered milk that has been opened on a shelf in a container with a tight-fitting lid for up to six months. If you open a large can or package of powdered milk, repackage it in smaller containers that can be tightly closed (glass jars or cans with tight-fitting lids are best) to keep out moisture. Powdered milk will absorb moisture and become lumpy when exposed to air. Nitrogen-packed nonfat powdered milk can be successfully stored for up to 5 years without any deterioration.

Helpful Hints for Using Powdered Milk

To chill reconstituted powdered milk:

- Refrigerate overnight before drinking to make it taste better.
- To chill it in a hurry, pour it into a large container and add a tray of ice. Shake gently back and forth until the milk is chilled. Remove the ice so it won't dilute the milk (or substitute some of the water with ice).

To improve the flavor of reconstituted powdered milk:

- If powdered milk has been stored a long time and the flavor has deteriorated, after reconstituting the milk, pour it back and forth between two pitchers or whip it in a blender or with electric beaters to incorporate more air into the milk.
- Add a small drop of vanilla to the milk to make it taste better.
- Mix it half and half with whole milk. This simple procedure to improve the flavor of dehydrated milk is the best way to rotate stored powdered milk.

To enrich fresh milk:

- Add 3 teaspoons of powdered milk to 1 cup whole milk. This increases its content of protein, B vitamins, calcium, and minerals.

To replace milk in cooking and baking:

- Replace regular milk with nonfat powdered milk to produce better browning in baked goods.
- Powdered milk can be sifted with dry ingredients for cakes and breads, stirred into flour for gravy and sauces, or mixed with cornstarch and sugar for puddings. Then add required amount of water to liquids in the recipe.
- In meat dishes, powdered milk adds tenderness and flavor by absorbing and holding meat juices. To enrich meatloafs or hamburgers, use 1/4 cup powdered milk for each pound of meat and mix well.
- In mashed potatoes, add 1/4 cup powdered milk for each cup of potatoes and the potato water for liquid to get the right consistency.
- Add 1/4 cup powdered milk to each cup of cooked cereal and water before cooking.

Making Other Dairy Products Using Powdered Milk

You can use powdered milk to make many of the dairy products you regularly use, such as evaporated milk, whipped topping, sweetened condensed milk, buttermilk, hot chocolate, and yogurt.

Evaporated Milk and Whipped Topping

1 cup water	Sugar to taste (for whipped
2/3 cup powdered milk	topping)
1/2 teaspoon lemon juice	
(for whipped topping)	

This will make a creamier milk that you can use to replace evaporated milk in any recipe. It also can be chilled and whipped into a topping by adding 1/2 teaspoon lemon juice. After it is whipped, fold in sugar to taste (about 1 tablespoon). Makes 1 cup.

Sweetened Condensed Milk

This recipe can be used in place of one 16-ounce can of sweetened condensed milk in any recipe, and you won't know the difference!

2 tablespoons butter	1/2 cup hot water
(or 2 tablespoons butter	3/4 cup non-instant powdered
powder reconstituted with	milk (or 1 1/3 cups instant)
a few drops water)	

Melt butter in hot water, then place hot mixture in blender. With blender going, add sugar and powdered milk; blend until smooth. Store up to 2 weeks in the refrigerator. Makes about 14 ounces.

Buttermilk

1 cup water	1 tablespoon vinegar or
1/4 cup powdered milk	lemon juice

Combine all ingredients and let mixture stand in a warm place until thickened (about 18 hours). Stir until smooth. Refrigerate. Makes 1 cup.

Cultured Buttermilk

You can purchase a buttermilk freeze-dried culture (see Resource Guide) and keep it indefinitely. Or you can make your own culture using this recipe.

1 cup powdered milk (or 13/4 cups instant powdered milk)	1/2 cup commercial or previously made buttermilk
3 cups slightly warm (not hot) water	Pinch of salt

Shake or beat all ingredients until blended. Cover and allow to stand at room temperature until curdled (6 to 12 hours). Refrigerate after curdling for as long as 2 to 3 weeks or freeze. Save 1/2 cup buttermilk to use as a starter for another quart. Use to replace buttermilk in any recipe or for drinking. Makes 1 quart.

Note: It will be necessary to use a fresh start of buttermilk occasionally.

Fudge-Flavored Hot Chocolate (Master Mix)

6 cups powdered milk	2 cups dry nondairy coffee
3 cups powdered sugar	creamer
1 cup unsweetened cocoa	1 1/2 large packages chocolate
powder	fudge pudding mix

Mix all ingredients together and keep in an airtight container. To use, mix 1 cup hot water to 1/3 cup hot chocolate mix. Makes 40 servings.

(Recipe from Carla Jean Meaders)

Yogurt

Yogurt is fermented milk. Bacterial microorganisms change the lactose of the milk into lactic acid, which acts as a preservative and keeps the milk palatable.

A yogurt starter is a must. You can purchase a plain unflavored yogurt, or a freeze-dried yogurt culture from the supermarket or health-food store, or see Resource Guide for ordering information. These starts can be used like a sourdough starter and fed every so often to keep them going indefinitely. Store the start in the freezer or use a plain commercial yogurt as a starter.

Instant Milk Yogurt

2 cups powdered milk	3 cups lukewarm water
2 tablespoons plain yogurt	

Place all ingredients in a blender and mix. Place in a warm area (preferably 110 degrees F) and let stand undisturbed until set (about 4 hours). If desired, place in jars and put the jars in hot water (110 degrees F) and cover to speed up the process. The cooler the temperature, the longer yogurt takes to set. At room temperature, the process can take days. Chill immediately when set; refrigerate for up to 4 weeks.

Reconstituting Powdered Butter and Shortening

You can use dry products to make a butter, margarine, or shortening substitute by following these simple recipes. Use the reconstituted mixture in any recipes calling for butter, margarine, or shortening. Note, however, that these reconstituted mixtures do *not* melt the way regular fats melt and cannot be used to fry foods. If you are not familiar with these products, I suggest that you purchase one can each to experiment with before stocking up.

Butter/Margarine

1 cup butter or margarine powder	1/2 teaspoon vegetable oil (optional)
2 tablespoons warm water	

Slowly mix butter or margarine powder with water until desired consistency is reached. To make the reconstituted butter or margarine taste better, add a small amount of vegetable oil (about 1/2 teaspoon) and blend until the desired consistency. Chill in your refrigerator. Makes 1 cup.

Shortening

1 cup shortening powder	1/2 teaspoon vegetable oil (optional)
1 tablespoon water	

Slowly mix shortening powder and water to the desired consistency, until it resembles shortening. A small amount of oil (about 1/2 teaspoon) can be added for texture and flavor. Reconstituted shortening powder can be used in any recipe that calls for shortening. The *unreconstituted* powder can be sprinkled on a griddle or skillet and it will melt. Makes 1/2 cup.

Grains

Instant Oatmeal Packets

1 1/2 cups instant oatmeal 1 cup powdered oats (see directions) 8 teaspoons powdered milk	8 teaspoons strawberry-apple bits 4 teaspoons sugar or sweet- ened drink mix (such as lemonade or strawberry)

To make powdered oats, blend 1 cup instant oatmeal in blender until powdery. Mix all ingredients together in a large bowl. Store mix in an airtight container. To make oatmeal, add 1 cup boiling water to 1/2 cup mix. Cook for 1 minute in a microwave or on the stove just until it thickens. Makes 6 (1/2-cup) servings.

Variations (each for one serving):
- Add 1 teaspoon apple bits and a pinch of cinnamon.
- Add 1 teaspoon brown sugar and a few raisins.
- Add 1 teaspoon dried peach-apple flakes and 1 tablespoon powdered milk.
- Add 1 teaspoon dried strawberries and 1 tablespoon powdered milk.

Quick Oatmeal

1 1/3 cups water 2/3 cup rolled oats	Pinch of salt

Bring the water to a full boil in saucepan. Add oats and salt; cook over medium heat until oats are thickened (about 2 minutes). Take pan off heat and stir contents. Serve with milk and honey as a breakfast cereal. Makes 1 serving.

9-Grain Master Mix

1 cup red wheat	1 cup grinding corn
1 cup white wheat	1 cup millet
1 cup rye	1 cup oats
1 cup barley	1 cup flax
1 cup buckwheat	

Combine all grains together into a master mix and store in an airtight container. When ready to use, grind it in a wheat grinder set on "crack." Makes 9 cups.

9-Grain Cracked Cereal

1^1/3 cups water	Pinch of salt
^{2}/3 cup 9-Grain Master Mix (see previous recipe)	

Bring water to a boil in saucepan. Add 9-Grain Master Mix and salt. Cook on medium heat until thick. Serve with milk and honey. Makes one serving.

Cornmeal Pancakes

2^1/4 cups water	1 cup powdered milk
2^1/2 tablespoons dried whole egg powder (or 1 egg)	1^1/2 cups cornmeal
2 tablespoons shortening powder (or 2 tablespoons regular shortening)	^{1}/4 cup flour
	1 teaspoon salt
	1 teaspoon sugar

Combine all ingredients and mix well. Let batter stand for 10 minutes to absorb the water. Pour small amount of batter onto a hot-oiled skillet. Brown on one side, then turn over and brown on the other side. Serve with honey butter and fruit such as strawberries or jam. Top with whipped topping if desired. Makes 6 to 8 pancakes.

Pasta

Macaroni and Cheese Casserole

1¹/₃ cups macaroni
4 cups boiling water (to cook
 macaroni in)
1 teaspoon salt
2 tablespoons dried green
 pepper
4 tablespoons dried parsley

2 teaspoons dried onion
¹/₂ cup dried cheese powder
²/₃ cup dried whole egg
 powder
6 tablespoons powdered milk
2 cups warm water

Cook macaroni in boiling salted water until tender. Drain and combine the macaroni and vegetables and place in a greased 9- by 13-inch pan. Mix together cheese, egg, milk, and warm water; blend well. Pour over the macaroni mixture. Bake at 350 degrees F for 50 minutes. Makes 4 servings.

Eggaroni

2 tablespoons butter
2 tablespoons white flour
¹/₂ cup powdered milk
2 cups warm water
9 hard-cooked eggs
6 tablespoons dried whole
 egg powder
¹/₂ cup chopped celery (or ¹/₄
 cup dried celery reconstituted with ¹/₂ cup water)

¹/₂ cup onion (or ¹/₄ cup dried
 onion reconstituted with
 ¹/₂ cup water)
1 teaspoon salt
³/₄ teaspoon marjoram
¹/₂ teaspoon pepper
2 cups cooked macaroni

Melt butter in a large saucepan; blend in flour and cook, stirring until mixture is smooth and boiling. Stir in powdered milk and 2 cups warm water. Bring to a boil, stirring constantly. Chop hard-cooked eggs. Stir chopped eggs and all remaining ingredients into milk mixture. Pour into greased 9- by 13-inch casserole pan. Bake at 350 degrees F for 35 to 40 minutes. Makes 6 (1-cup) servings.

Macaroni and Cheese

4 cups dry macaroni
8 cups water (to cook
   macaroni in)
1 teaspoon salt
1 1/2 cups cheese blend

1 (8-ounce) can cream of
   mushroom soup
3 cups water
Salt and pepper to taste

Cook macaroni by boiling in 8 cups water and 1 teaspoon salt in saucepan until tender. Drain cooking water and rinse macaroni with fresh warm water. In a separate pan, add dried cheese powder, cream of mushroom soup, and 3 cups water; blend well. Cook over low heat until the cheese sauce is thick and free of lumps. Add cooked macaroni and salt and pepper to taste. Makes 4 servings.

Homemade Egg Noodles
(Whole Wheat or White)

1 2/3 cups dried whole egg
   powder
2 cups sifted flour (wheat or
   white)

1 1/2 teaspoons salt
3/4 cup water
1/2 cup spinach, dried or fresh
   (optional)

Sift dry ingredients together. Add water to dry ingredients and mix well. Add spinach if desired. (If using dried spinach, reconstitute first.) Knead dough lightly. Divide into 4 pieces. Roll each piece very thin on a floured board. Cut rolled-out dough into strips 3 inches wide. Stack the strips and slice into 1/4-inch widths. Spread out on waxed paper and dry thoroughly at room temperature. When dry, use or store the noodles immediately because dried whole egg powder is activated when mixed with water and is subject to salmonella poisoning when left out. Store in a covered container in the refrigerator or freezer.

To cook the noodles: Cook dry noodles in boiling salted water or broth. Cover and cook slowly for 12 minutes. Makes about 1 pound dry noodles.

Rice

Rice is another important staple for long-term food storage. It is also a versatile ingredient that complements a variety of foods and flavors.

Mushroom, Chicken, and Rice Casserole

1 tablespoon butter	1 (10-ounce) can cream of
1 cup uncooked rice	mushroom soup
1 cut-up fryer or package of	2 cups milk (or 1/2 cup pow-
chicken breasts, sliced (or	dered milk reconstituted
1 cup chicken TVP reconsti-	with 2 cups water)
tuted with 2 cups water)	1 teaspoon parsley flakes
1 package dried onion soup	1/2 teaspoon paprika

Place rice in the bottom of a 9- by 13-inch casserole pan greased with butter. Lay chicken pieces (or TVP) on top of the rice. Sprinkle with the onion soup mix. Combine mushroom soup and milk, blend well to remove lumps, and pour over the rice and chicken. Bake, covered, at 300 degrees F for 2 1/2 hours. Sprinkle with parsley and paprika before serving. Makes 4 servings.

Baked Rice

2 cups brown rice	1 tablespoon instant chicken
3 cups boiling water	or beef bouillon
Salt (optional)	

Preheat oven to 350 degrees F. Toast rice in dry pan until golden brown. Put toasted rice in an ovenproof dish. Mix bouillon with boiling water and pour over toasted rice. Add a pinch of salt. Bake for 40 to 45 minutes. Add a little more water during baking if necessary. Makes 4 servings.

Tips for Using Rice

- Do not rinse rice before cooking. When rice is processed, the hull is removed and there are valuable nutrients on the surface of the processed rice. Rinsing will wash away these nutrients.
- Add the correct amount of water. If you add too much water, the rice will be sticky and clump together.
- Do not stir rice while it is cooking. This will break the pieces of rice and it won't be light and fluffy.
- Do not lift the lid of the rice pan while it is cooking because it lets out steam and will cause the rice to become dry.
- When cooking rice, the water called for in any recipe can be substituted with other liquids such as beef or chicken broth or bouillon. Tomato juice can also be used for a great flavor.
- Reconstituted dried vegetables such as dried sweet peas, mushrooms, carrots, celery, onions, and any other can be added to rice. Bacon bits and grated cheese are good mixed in with rice.
- Rice is excellent with any kind of gravy or sauce over the top of it. Mix in a little TVP meat substitute such as beef- or sausage-flavored TVP.
- Rice can be reheated in the microwave oven or in a pan on the stove. Add a small amount of water and warm it over medium heat.

Skillet Spanish Rice

1 pound lean ground beef
(or 1 cup beef-flavored TVP
reconstituted with 2 cups
water)
1 cup chopped onions (or 1/2
cup dried onion reconsti-
tuted with 1 cup water)
1/2 cup diced green sweet pepper (or 1/4 cup dried green
pepper reconstituted with
1/2 cup water)

1 cup uncooked rice
1 teaspoon chili powder
1/2 teaspoon seasoning salt
1/2 teaspoon ground cumin
1/2 teaspoon black pepper
1 (8-ounce) can tomato sauce
(or 1 cup tomato powder
reconstituted with 1 1/2 cups
water)
1 1/2 cups water

Cook beef or TVP, onion, and sweet pepper in large skillet over medium heat; drain fat. (If you are reconstituting dried vegetables and TVP, add the stated amount of water first to reconstitute them.) Stir in remaining ingredients and 1 1/2 cups water; bring to a boil. Reduce heat, cover, and simmer 15 to 20 minutes or until rice is tender. Makes 8 servings.

Mexican-Style Rice

2 tablespoons butter
1 1/4 cups rice, uncooked
1/2 cup chopped onion (or 1/4
cup dried onion reconsti-
tuted with 1/2 cup water)
1/4 cup chopped green pepper
(or 1/8 cup dried green

pepper reconstituted with
1/4 cup water)
1 clove garlic, minced
2 cups hot water
1 (16-ounce) can tomatoes,
chopped and undrained
1/2 teaspoon chili powder

In a large saucepan, melt butter and add rice, onion, pepper, and garlic. Cook over low heat, stirring constantly until rice is brown. Add remaining ingredients. Cover and cook over low heat until liquid is absorbed (about 35 minutes). Makes 6 (1-cup) servings.

Oriental Fried Rice

5 cups cooked white or brown rice

4 eggs (or 1/2 cup dried whole egg powder reconstituted with 1/2 cup water)

1 teaspoon salt

1 teaspoon garlic seasoning

1/4 cup butter (or 1/4 cup butter powder reconstituted with 1 1/2 teaspoons water)

1 cup mung bean (or other) sprouts

1/2 cup peas (or 1/4 cup dried peas reconstituted with 1/2 cup water)

1 cup sliced mushrooms (or 1/2 cup dried mushrooms reconstituted with 1 cup water)

2 cups diced chicken (or 1 cup chicken-flavored TVP reconstituted with 2 cups water)

Beat eggs and spices with fork until blended. In skillet, mix cooked rice with egg and spice mixture. Cook over low heat, stirring until eggs are cooked. Remove from heat. Add butter, sprouts, peas, mushrooms, and chicken; stir gently. Do not allow mushrooms and sprouts to cook all the way through. Serve immediately. Makes 8 servings.

Sauces and Gravies

Staples such as pasta, rice, and potatoes are bland unless carefully seasoned or served with an accompanying sauce. This section focuses on the sauces and gravies that make plain foods palatable.

Basic White Sauce

3 tablespoons butter	1 cup milk (or 1/4 cup pow-
3 tablespoons all-purpose	dered milk reconstituted
white flour	with 1 cup water)
	1/4 teaspoon salt

Over low heat, melt butter in a saucepan. Add flour. Blend until smooth. Add milk at once and cook until thick, stirring constantly so it won't burn. If the sauce is too thick, stir in more milk until it is the desired consistency. Add salt. To make a cheese sauce, add 1/2 cup grated cheddar cheese (or use following recipe). Makes 1 cup.

(Recipe from Cookin' with Home Storage)

Cheese Sauce

1 cup hot water	1 teaspoon dried onion
1/2 cup cheese blend powder	1 teaspoon sugar
(or 1/2 cup grated cheddar	2 tablespoons butter
cheese)	(or 2 tablespoons butter
1/4 cup powdered milk	powder reconstituted with a
1 1/2 teaspoons cornstarch	few drops water) (optional)
1 cup water	

Gradually combine cheese blend with hot water, stirring until smooth and creamy. Add remaining ingredients and cook on low heat to warm. To make creamier, add butter (or butter powder). Makes 2 cups.

Basic Milk Gravy

1 cup powdered milk	1/2 teaspoon salt
3 cups water	1 tablespoon butter
3 heaping tablespoons all-purpose white flour	Bacon bits and drippings or TVP bacon bits (optional)

Mix the powdered milk and water (or substitute 3 cups whole milk for powdered milk and water). Add flour and salt, stirring constantly. Cook over medium heat until the gravy is thickened. Add butter and stir again until smooth. For great flavor, add crumbled bacon and drippings (or TVP bacon bits). Makes 3 cups.

(*Recipe from* Cookin' with Home Storage)

Chicken Gravy

1 1/2 tablespoons butter	1/4 cup instant powdered milk
1 tablespoon all-purpose white flour	1 teaspoon onion powder
1 1/2 tablespoons instant chicken bouillon	1/2 teaspoon garlic powder
1 1/4 cups water	1/4 teaspoon turmeric

Melt butter in pan. Add flour, cooking until it thickens. Mix dried milk with water. Stir milk into butter and flour mixture. Add remaining spices and stir until thick and creamy. Makes 1 1/2 cups.

(*Recipe from* Cookin' with Home Storage)

Onion Gravy

1/4 cup butter
1 tablespoon all-purpose
    white flour
1/4 cup cold water
1 tablespoon instant beef
    bouillon

2 tablespoons cornstarch
2 cups boiling water
3 cups chopped onion
Salt and pepper to taste

Melt butter in pan. In separate container, mix flour with 1/4 cup cold water; blend until smooth. Stir in bouillon, cornstarch, and 2 cups boiling water. Add mixture to melted butter in pan, stirring constantly until thick, smooth, and bubbly. Stir in onions, salt, and pepper. Makes 3 cups.

(Recipe from Cookin' with Home Storage)

Beef Gravy

1 1/2 tablespoons butter
1 tablespoon all-purpose
    white flour
1 teaspoon minced onion
    powder (or 3 teaspoons
    fresh onion, minced)

1 teaspoon Worcestershire
    sauce
1 1/4 cups water
1 1/2 tablespoons instant beef
    bouillon

Melt butter in saucepan over low heat; add flour, stirring until thick. Add remaining ingredients, blending until thick and creamy. Makes 1 1/2 cups.

(Recipe from Cookin' with Home Storage)

RECIPES USING STORED FOODS

Herb Gravy

1 tablespoon butter	1 tablespoon parsley
4 1/2 tablespoons all-purpose	Pinch of thyme
white flour	1 teaspoon chives
1 (16-ounce) can chicken or	1/2 teaspoon salt
beef broth	Pepper to taste

Melt butter with 1 tablespoon flour in saucepan. In separate bowl, mix remaining flour with a small amount of water and blend; add to melted butter with remaining ingredients. Cook over medium heat until thick and smooth. Makes 2 cups.

(Recipe from Cookin' with Home Storage)

Tomato Paste

1 cup dried tomato powder	1/2 teaspoon sugar
1 1/2 cups water	

Combine all ingredients in saucepan. Simmer on warm until the paste thickens. Stir until smooth and creamy. Makes 1 1/2 cups.

(Recipe from Cookin' with Home Storage)

Tomato Sauce

1 cup dried tomato powder	1 teaspoon garlic powder
2 cups water	1/2 teaspoon salt
1/2 teaspoon sugar	Pepper to taste
2 tablespoons dried minced	
onion	

Combine all ingredients in a saucepan and simmer over medium heat until tomato sauce thickens. Stir or blend until creamy. Makes 2 cups.

(Recipe from Cookin' with Home Storage)

Tomato Juice

1 cup dried tomato powder
5 cups water
1/2 teaspoon sugar
2 tablespoons dried minced
   onion

1 teaspoon garlic powder
Salt, pepper, lemon juice to
   taste

Combine all ingredients in a saucepan and simmer over medium heat until onions are tender (about 10 minutes). Makes 5 cups.

Tomato Soup

1 cup dried tomato powder
2 1/2 cups water
1/2 cup powdered milk
1/2 teaspoon sugar

2 tablespoons dried onion
1 teaspoon garlic powder
Salt and pepper to taste

Combine all ingredients in saucepan and simmer over low heat for 10 minutes or until soup thickens. Stir until creamy. Makes 2 1/2 cups.

Spaghetti Sauce

3/4 teaspoon packaged Italian
   seasoning mix
1 teaspoon sugar
1/2 teaspoon minced garlic or
   garlic salt
1 1/2 teaspoons salt
2 teaspoons chopped dried
   green pepper

1 tablespoon cornstarch
1 tablespoon parsley flakes
1 tablespoon dried minced
   onion
1 cup tomato paste (or 1 cup
   tomato powder reconstituted with 1 1/2 cups water)
1 1/2 cups water

Mix all ingredients together and simmer for 20 minutes over medium heat. Makes 2 1/2 cups.

RECIPES USING STORED FOODS

Cheese Spread

3/4 cup cheese blend powder | 3/4 cup water
2 tablespoons butter |

Gradually combine cheese blend and butter with hot water, stirring until smooth and creamy. Cook on low heat to warm. Makes 3/4 cup.

Soups

These recipes are based on using dehydrated foods (not freeze-dried) common to most food storage programs. Most of them start with one of the two wonderful bases that follow.

Creamy Chicken Base

1/2 cup powdered milk | 1/4 cup all-purpose white flour
1/8 cup instant chicken | 1/8 cup butter powder
   bouillon | 6 cups water

Mix all ingredients together and use in soup recipes calling for Creamy Chicken Base. Makes 6 cups.

Beefy Tomato Base

1/4 cup instant beef bouillon | 6 cups water
1/4 cup tomato powder |

Mix all ingredients together and use in soup recipes calling for Beefy Tomato Base. Makes 6 cups.

Traditional Potato Corn Chowder

1 recipe Creamy Chicken Base
  (recipe on page 251)
3/4 cup dried potato flakes
1/4 cup dried whole kernel
  corn
2 tablespoons dried onion
  flakes

Salt and pepper to taste
Pinch of garlic powder
  (optional)
Pinch of white pepper
  (optional)
1/4 cup dried potato dices

Mix all ingredients in a saucepan and bring to a boil. Turn down heat and simmer for 25 minutes. Makes 6 cups.

Broccoli and Cheddar Soup

1 recipe Creamy Chicken Base
  (recipe on page 251)
1/4 cup dried broccoli florets
1/4 cup cheddar cheese
  powder

2 teaspoons dried onion flakes
Salt and pepper to taste
1/2 cup instant rice (optional)

Mix all ingredients in a saucepan and bring to a boil. Turn down heat and simmer for 25 minutes. Makes 6 cups.

Creamy Garden Vegetable Soup

1 recipe Creamy Chicken Base
  (recipe on page251)
1/2 cup dried potato flakes
2/3 cup any one or a mix of
  dried vegetables, such as
  peas, carrots, diced potato,
  green beans, corn

Salt and pepper to taste
1 teaspoon dried parsley
  (optional)
1/2 cup elbow macaroni and
  1/2 cup water (optional)

Mix all ingredients in a saucepan and bring to a boil. Turn down heat and simmer for 25 minutes. Makes 6 cups.

Heartland Potato Bacon Soup

1 recipe Creamy Chicken Base (recipe on page 251)	Salt and pepper to taste
1 cup dried potato dices or flakes	Pinch of garlic powder (optional)
1/4 cup bacon bits TVP	Dash of "smoke" or "grill" flavoring (optional)
2 teaspoons dried onion flakes	

Mix all ingredients in a saucepan and bring to a boil. Turn down the heat and simmer for 25 minutes. Makes 6 cups.

Traditional Italian Minestrone Soup

1 recipe Beefy Tomato Base (recipe on page 251)	1 tablespoon dried sweet peas
3/4 cup pasta (elbow macaroni)	1 tablespoon dried green beans
1/2 cup precooked dried beans (navy, black, pinto, or kidney)	1/8 cup dried potato dices
1/8 cup cornmeal	Pinch each of garlic, parsley, oregano, and basil
1 tablespoon dried onion flakes	Salt to taste
1 tablespoon dried carrot dices	1 teaspoon olive oil (optional)
	1 bay leaf
	1/2 cup beef-flavored TVP

Mix all ingredients together in a saucepan and bring to a boil. Turn down heat and simmer for 25 minutes. Makes 6 cups.

Meatless Chili Soup

1 recipe Beefy Tomato Base
(recipe on page 251)
1 cup precooked dried beans
(navy, black, pinto, or kidney)
1/2 cup pasta (elbow macaroni)
1/8 cup chili powder
1 tablespoon onion powder
1 tablespoon barley, flaked or
pearl

1 tablespoon dried green or
red bell pepper dices
1 teaspoon sugar
Pinch of garlic powder
Large pinch of baking soda
Salt and pepper to taste
3/4 cup beef-flavored TVP
(optional)

Mix all ingredients together in a saucepan and bring to a boil. Turn down heat and simmer for 25 minutes. Makes 6 cups.

Hearty Beans and Rice Soup

1 recipe Beefy Tomato Base
(recipe on page 251)
3/4 cup precooked dried
beans (navy, black, pinto,
or kidney)
1/2 cup long-grain rice
1 tablespoon barley, flaked or
pearl
1 tablespoon dried carrot
dices
1 tablespoon cornmeal
1/8 cup dried potato dices

1 tablespoon dried sweet peas
2 teaspoons dried onion flakes
1 tablespoon dried red or
green bell pepper dices
1 tablespoon dried celery
Salt and pepper to taste
1/8 teaspoon parsley, 1/8 teaspoon basil, or 1 bay leaf
(optional)
3/4 cup beef-flavored TVP
(optional)

Mix all ingredients together in a saucepan and bring to a boil. Turn down heat and simmer for 25 minutes. Makes 6 cups.

Scottish Homeland Barley Soup

1 recipe Beefy Tomato Base
(recipe on page 251)
1/8 cup barley, flaked or pearl
3/4 cup dried potato dices
1/2 cup precooked dried beans
(navy, black, pinto, or kidney)
1 tablespoon dried sweet peas
1 tablespoon all-purpose
white flour
1 tablespoon dried carrot dices
1 tablespoon cornmeal

2 teaspoons dried onion flakes
1 tablespoon dried red or
green bell pepper dices
Pinch of dried parsley
Salt and pepper to taste
Pinch of garlic powder
(optional)
Dash of "smoke" or "grill"
flavoring (optional)
3/4 cup beef-flavored TVP
(optional)

Mix all ingredients together in a saucepan and bring to a boil. Turn down heat and simmer for 25 minutes. Makes 6 cups.

Grandma's Chicken Noodle Soup

You can make fantastic-tasting chicken noodle soup using a chicken bouillon base.

6 cups water
1/4 cup instant chicken
bouillon
1 cup pasta of your choice
1/8 cup barley, flaked or pearl
1/4 cup dried potato dices
2 tablespoons dried sweet
peas
2 tablespoons dried carrot
dices

1 tablespoon all-purpose
white flour
1 tablespoon dried onion
flakes
2 teaspoons dried celery
Salt and pepper to taste
Pinch of white pepper
(optional)
3/4 cup chicken-flavored TVP
(optional)

Mix all ingredients in a saucepan and bring to a boil. Turn down heat and simmer for 25 minutes. Makes 6 cups.

Cream Soup Base

2 tablespoons salad oil	3 1/4 cups water
2 tablespoons white flour	1/2 teaspoon salt
2 tablespoons butter powder (or	3/4 cup powdered milk
2 tablespoons fresh butter)	

Blend flour with oil in saucepan. Add butter or butter powder. Stir in all remaining ingredients and cook on low heat until thickened. Use as base for various cream soups, such as those listed below. Makes 3 cups.

(*Recipe from* Cookin' with Food Storage)

Cream Soup Variations:

- **Cream of Celery Soup**: Add 1 cup celery (or 1/2 cup dried celery reconstituted with 1/2 cup water) and 1 tablespoon minced onion (or 1/2 tablespoon dried onion reconstituted with 1/2 tablespoon water).

- **Cream of Mushroom**: Add 1 cup mushrooms (or 1/2 cup dried mushrooms reconstituted with 1/2 cup water) and 1 tablespoon minced onion (or 1 tablespoon dried onion reconstituted with 1 tablespoon water).

- **Cream of Chicken Soup**: Add 1 cup chicken (cut into small pieces) and 1 tablespoon minced onion (or 1/2 tablespoon dried onion reconstituted with 1/2 tablespoon water).

- **Cream of Corn Soup**: Add 1 (16-ounce) can cream-style corn (or 3/4 cup dried corn reconstituted with 2 1/4 cups water) and 1 tablespoon chopped onions (or 1/2 tablespoon dried onion reconstituted with 1/2 tablespoon water); Season with pepper.

- **Cream of Bean Soup**: Add 3 cups cooked dried beans, 4 teaspoons chopped onion (or 2 teaspoons dried onion reconstituted with 2 teaspoons water) and 4 teaspoons peppers (or 2 teaspoons dried peppers reconstituted with 2 teaspoons water).

- **Cream of Onion Soup:** Add 2½ cups chopped onions (or 1¼ cups dried onion reconstituted with 1¼ cups water). Add salt and pepper to taste.

- **Cream of Broccoli Soup:** Add 2 cups chopped broccoli (or 1 cup dried broccoli reconstituted with 2 cups water). Season with onion, salt, and pepper.

- Add any variation of vegetables, cheese, or meat; serve over rice or whole grain.

Note: You can use either fresh or dehydrated vegetables. If using dried vegetables, reconstitute before putting them in the soup by adding enough water to cover and letting them stand until all water is absorbed. Use as you would fresh vegetables.

French Cream of Onion Soup

¼ cup powdered milk reconstituted with 4 cups water	1 egg yolk, beaten (or 1 tablespoon dried whole egg powder reconstituted with 1 tablespoon water)
1 cup dried minced onion	
1 tablespoon butter	
¼ cup all-purpose white flour	Salt to taste
2 chicken bouillon cubes	¼ cup grated cheese (optional)
2 cups water	½ cup dried bread crumbs or croutons (optional)

Reconstitute powdered milk by mixing with 4 cups water. Sauté onions in butter. Stir in the flour and cook over low heat until smooth and bubbly. Stir in reconstituted milk. Continue cooking until the mixture is slightly thickened. Dissolve bouillon in 2 cups water. Add to milk mixture and stir. Cook 5 more minutes; remove from the heat. Stir small amounts of egg yolk into soup. Season with salt to taste. If desired, place grated cheese on the bottom of the bowl before adding the soup and top with dried bread crumbs or croutons. Makes 6 cups.

(Recipe from Cookin' with Food Storage)

Cream of Potato Soup

1 1/2 cups cubed potatoes (or 1/2 cup dried potato dices reconstituted with 3 cups water)	1 tablespoon butter (or 1 tablespoon butter powder reconstituted with a few drops water)
1 tablespoon chopped onion (or 1 1/2 teaspoons dried onion reconstituted with 1 1/2 teaspoons water)	1 tablespoon flour
	1 tablespoon instant chicken bouillon
3/4 teaspoon salt	1/2 cup powdered milk
	2 3/4 cups water

Cook the potatoes, onion, and salt in saucepan until tender. (For dried potatoes, first mix with 3 cups boiling water in saucepan and let stand until reconstituted.) Blend the butter (or reconstituted butter powder) and flour together; stir into hot potato mixture. Stir constantly until mixture thickens. Add bouillon, powdered milk, and water; reheat. Season with salt and pepper to taste. Makes 6 cups.

Cream of Tomato Soup

2 cups canned tomatoes (no juice)	**White Sauce**
1 small diced onion (or 3 tablespoons dried onion)	1 cube butter
	1/2 cup all-purpose white flour
1/4 teaspoon pepper	1/2 cup powdered milk
2 teaspoons brown sugar	2 cups water

Simmer first four ingredients for 15 minutes, until thick. In a separate pan, make the white sauce by melting butter and adding the flour until a thick paste forms. In separate container, mix powdered milk and water together, then blend in with flour paste. Continue to cook, stirring until thick. Add tomato mixture and stir well. Makes 4 servings.

(Recipe from Cookin' with Food Storage*)*

Bean Chowder

3/4 cup dry beans	1 1/2 teaspoons all-purpose
3 cups water	white flour
1 1/2 teaspoons salt	1 tablespoon butter
3/4 cup diced potatoes	(or 1 tablespoon butter
(or 1/4 cup dried potato	powder reconstituted with
dices reconstituted with	a few drops water)
3/4 cup water)	3/4 cup canned tomatoes
1/2 cup chopped onion (or	1/3 cup bell pepper
1/4 cup dried onion reconsti-	(or 2 tablespoons dried bell
tuted with 1/4 cup water)	pepper reconstituted with
3/8 cup powdered milk recon-	2 tablespoons water)
stituted with 1 1/2 cups water	

Soak the beans overnight; drain. Add 3 cups water and salt; boil about 1 hour, covering with a lid until beans are almost done. Add remaining ingredients; cook over low heat about 10 more minutes, until thickened. Serve hot. Makes 6 servings.

(Recipe from Cookin' with Food Storage)

Sweet Corn Chowder

1 1/4 cups dried sweet corn	2 tablespoons bacon bits TVP
2 teaspoons dried onion	1 teaspoon salt
3 3/4 cups water	1/8 teaspoon pepper
1 cup powdered milk reconsti-	2 tablespoons all-purpose
tuted with 4 cups water	white flour
2 tablespoons oil	

Soak corn and onion in 3 3/4 cups water until reconstituted. Add milk, oil, bacon bits, salt, and pepper. Bring to a boil, reduce heat, and simmer 30 minutes. Mix flour in a small amount of water and slowly add to the soup to thicken it. Cook on low until soup thickens and the corn is tender (about 15 minutes longer). Makes 5 cups.

(Recipe from Cookin' with Food Storage)

New England Style Clam Chowder

1 cup finely chopped onion (or 1/2 cup dried onion reconstituted with 1/2 cup water)

1 cup celery (or 1/2 cup dried celery reconstituted with 1/2 cup water)

2 cups diced potatoes (or 3/4 cup dried potato dices reconstituted with 2 1/4 cups water)

2 (4-ounce) cans clams

3/4 cup butter

3/4 cup all-purpose white flour

1 cup powdered milk reconstituted with 4 cups water

1 1/2 teaspoons salt

Pepper to taste

1/2 cup cooked crumbled bacon

Place onion, celery, and potatoes in a pan. Drain the juice from the canned clams and add clams to vegetables, adding enough water to cover. Simmer for 20 minutes. In another pan, melt butter. Add flour, blend, and cook 1 to 2 minutes. Stir in milk until smooth and thick. Add to undrained vegetables and clams. Add salt and pepper to taste. Stir in bacon. Makes 6 servings.

Split Pea Soup

1 cup dried split peas

3 1/2 cups water

2 tablespoons chopped onions (or 2 tablespoons dried onion reconstituted with 2 tablespoons water)

2 tablespoons diced carrots (or 1 tablespoon dried diced carrots reconstituted with 1 tablespoon water)

2 teaspoons diced celery (or 1 teaspoon dried diced celery reconstituted with 1 teaspoon water)

1 teaspoon salt

Sort dried peas, removing any rocks or dirt clods, and rinse well. Add to soup pot along with water and vegetables; bring to a boil. Reduce heat and simmer for 1 1/2 hours, or until the peas are tender. Add salt to taste. Makes 6 servings.

Beefy Barley Soup

8 cups water
4 teaspoons instant beef
  bouillon
1 cup dried barley
1 cup chopped onion (or 1/2
  cup dried onion reconstituted with 1/2 cup water)
1/4 cup fresh chopped carrots
  (or 2 tablespoons dried
  chopped carrots reconstituted with 4 tablespoons
  water)
1/4 cup fresh diced celery (or 2
  tablespoons dried chopped
  celery reconstituted with
  2 tablespoons water)
2 teaspoons dried oregano
2 teaspoons dried parsley
1 bay leaf
Salt and pepper to taste

In a medium saucepan, bring the water and bouillon to a boil. Add remaining ingredients except salt and pepper. Return to a boil. Lower temperature and simmer for about 1 hour or until barley is tender. Add a little more water if necessary. Add salt and pepper to taste. Makes 6 servings.

TVP (Textured Vegetable Protein)

TVP is a product made from soybeans. It is considered a meat substitute because the protein content is similar to that of meat, yet people on a vegetarian diet can use TVP.

TVP comes in several flavors, the most common of which are plain, taco, beef, chicken, and bacon bits. Other flavors include barbecue, sausage, ham, pepperoni, sloppy Joe, and pork. Plain TVP can be flavored with either chicken or beef bouillon.

To reconstitute, add 1 cup TVP to 2 cups of water. Cook it in a frying pan until all the water is absorbed. The TVP will double in bulk and resemble ground beef, chopped chicken, or ham. However, TVP is blander than meat so it requires about twice the amount of seasonings as you would use for meat. TVP will absorb or take on any flavor of spices or meat with which it is cooked. Use 1 tablespoon or 1 cube bouillon per cup of TVP product to add flavor.

TVP will store unopened for three to five years. Once opened, it should be used within a year. TVP can be added directly in dry form to soup or other recipes that have ample liquids in them. Just add the extra water to the soup.

TVP can be added to any recipe that calls for meat. It can also be combined with other meat to stretch your food budget. Try it in casseroles. Or try adding ham-flavored TVP, sausage-flavored TVP, or TVP bacon bits to scrambled eggs or omelets. Bacon bits are great as a salad topping or in clam chowder. Ham-flavored TVP can be added to beans for a great flavor. Pepperoni-flavored TVP can be used as a topping for pizza. Use your imagination and substitute TVP in any recipe calling for meat.

Beef Casserole

1/2 cup dried mushrooms re-constituted in 1 cup water	1 teaspoon instant beef bouillon
1 1/2 cups cooked rice	1 (8-ounce) can cream of mushroom soup
1 cup water	2 cups water
1 cup beef-flavored TVP	1/2 cup grated cheddar cheese (optional)
1 tablespoon dried onion	

Reconstitute dried mushrooms by soaking them in 1 cup of water for one hour. Drain and chop mushrooms and set aside for sauce. In a medium-sized skillet, combine 1 cup water, beef-flavored TVP, and onions. Cook them over medium heat for 10 minutes until tender. In a 9- by 13-inch casserole dish, layer half the rice then follow with half the TVP burger mixture. Add another layer until all is used.

To make sauce, combine the reconstituted mushrooms, bouillon, cream of mushroom soup, and 2 cups water. Cook over medium heat and stir until smooth and thick. Pour over the casserole, then bake at 450 degrees F for 20 minutes. If desired, sprinkle cheese on top of the hot casserole. Makes 4 servings.

Potato Beef Casserole

1 cup mashed potato flakes	2 tablespoons dried onion
1 teaspoon salt	3 cups water
3 cups boiling water	1 cup grated cheddar cheese
1 1/2 cups beef-flavored TVP	

Beat mashed potato flakes, salt, and 3 cups boiling water for 2 minutes or until fluffy; set aside. Simmer TVP, onion, and 3 cups water in a skillet until onion is tender and all the water is absorbed. (The TVP can be mixed half and half with hamburger, if desired.) Place the TVP mixture in a 9- by 13-inch casserole dish. Spread mashed potatoes on the top of TVP/hamburger. Top potatoes with cheese and bake for 15 minutes at 450 degrees F, until potatoes and cheese are brown. Makes 6 servings.

Beef Stew

2 tablespoons instant beef bouillon	1 cup diced fresh carrots (or 1/2 cup dried carrots reconstituted with 1 cup water)
4 cups cooked hamburger (or 2 cups beef-flavored TVP)	2 cups diced fresh potatoes (or 1 cup dried potato dices reconstituted with 3 cups water)
1/4 cup tomato powder	
2 tablespoons fresh onion (or 1 tablespoon dried onion reconstituted with 1 tablespoon water)	1 cup fresh peas (or 1/2 cup dried sweet peas reconstituted with 1 cup water)
1 teaspoon garlic pepper	12 cups water
2 1/2 teaspoons salt	

Combine all ingredients in a soup pot. Cover with a lid and boil. Turn the stove down to medium-low heat and simmer for 30 minutes. To thicken the stew, mix 3 tablespoons all-purpose white flour with 1/2 cup of water and slowly pour into the stew until it thickens. Serve over cooked rice, wheat, or other grains if desired. Makes 10 servings.

TVP Sausage Gravy over Biscuits

1 cup sausage-flavored TVP	2 teaspoons rubbed sage
2 1/2 cups hot water	1 teaspoon marjoram
1/4 cup butter	1/2 teaspoon salt
1/4 cup all-purpose white flour	1/4 teaspoon pepper
4 cups milk (or 1 cup pow- dered milk reconstituted with 4 cups water)	

Reconstitute sausage-flavored TVP in hot water and cook in a skillet until water is absorbed; set aside. (If using fresh sausage, fry in skillet until crumbled and cooked; drain grease.) In a separate skillet, melt butter and add flour. Cook mixture until slightly browned. Add milk and spices and stir until gravy is thickened and free of lumps. Add TVP or sausage to the gravy. Excellent over toast or homemade biscuits (see recipe for Whole Wheat Biscuits on page 210). Makes 6 to 8 servings.

Tacos

1 cup cooked kidney or pinto beans	2 cups cooked rice
	1 1/2 cups taco-flavored TVP
1 cup hot water	1 tablespoon dried onion
1 teaspoon instant chicken bouillon	(or 2 tablespoons fresh finely chopped onions)
1/2 cup dried sweet corn re- constituted with 1 1/2 cups water (or 1 cup frozen corn)	1 1/2 cups water
	6 taco shells

Combine first five ingredients and simmer until the water is gone. In a separate skillet, combine taco-flavored TVP, dried onion, and 1 1/2 cups water. Cook until all water is absorbed and mixture is slightly browned. Add to the beans, rice, and corn mixture. Stir and serve hot in taco shells. Makes 6 servings.

Beef and Cheese Macaroni

1 cup beef-flavored TVP	2 teaspoons salt
1 tablespoon dried onion	1 (15-ounce) can cream-style
1 cup water	corn
1/3 cup tomato powder	1 cup uncooked macaroni
1 1/4 cups water	1/4 cup dried cheese blend

Combine TVP, dried onion, and 1 cup water in a skillet and cook over medium heat until it resembles hamburger. Combine the remaining ingredients and mix with TVP. Put into 9- by 13-inch casserole dish; cover with foil or lid and bake at 300 degrees F for 1 hour. Makes 6 servings.

Chicken and Noodles

12 ounces fettuccini noodles	2 1/2 tablespoons all-purpose
1 teaspoon salt	white flour
1 cup dried mushrooms recon-	1 1/2 cups water
stituted with 1 cup water (or	3/4 cup powdered milk
2 cups fresh sliced mush-	1 teaspoon instant chicken
rooms)	bouillon
2 tablespoons oil (for sautée-	1/2 cup chicken-flavored TVP
ing mushrooms)	reconstituted with 1 cup
4 1/2 tablespoons butter	water
powder	1/4 cup dried cheese blend
4 1/2 tablespoons water	

Break up the noodles into 3-inch pieces; boil in salted water until tender. Drain the noodles and place them in a buttered 9- by 13-inch casserole dish. In a separate pan, sauté mushrooms in 2 tablespoons oil. Combine butter powder, flour, and 4 1/2 tablespoons water with the mushrooms. Cook until mixture forms a thick paste. Combine 1 1/2 cups water, powdered milk, and bouillon together; add to mushroom paste. Add cooked TVP; stir until thickened. Pour sauce over noodles and sprinkle with the cheese blend. Bake at 350 degrees F for 15 minutes or until it bubbles. Makes 4 to 6 servings.

TVP Veggie Burgers

1 cup beef- or chicken-flavored TVP
3/4 cup hot water
1 tablespoon ketchup (or 1 tablespoon dried tomato powder reconstituted with 1 tablespoon water)
1 teaspoon salt
1/2 teaspoon garlic powder
1/2 teaspoon marjoram
1/2 teaspoon oregano
1/8 cup dried carrots (or 1/4 cup fresh grated carrot)
1/8 cup dried celery (or 1/4 cup finely chopped fresh celery)
2 tablespoons dried onion (or 4 tablespoons finely chopped fresh onion)
1 tablespoon dried parsley
1/2 cup hot water
1/4 cup whole wheat flour
4 tablespoons vegetable oil or butter

Combine first seven ingredients; let mixture stand in a bowl until it thickens. In a separate bowl, combine the remaining ingredients and let stand until reconstituted. (If using fresh vegetables instead of dried, eliminate the reconstitution water.) When all the ingredients are reconstituted, combine TVP spice mixture with vegetable mixture and stir well. Form into patties. Fry the patties in a skillet in oil or butter. When brown, turn them over and brown the other side. Serve just like hamburgers for a delicious meatless variation! Makes 6 servings.

RESOURCE GUIDE

Where do you purchase whole grains, beans, rice, and other dehydrated and freeze-dried foods, as well as wheat grinders, bread makers, canning and sprouting supplies, and all the other food storage supplies mentioned in this book? I suggest you start by looking in the yellow pages of your telephone directory under Grain Dealers, Health Food Stores, Dehydrated Food Suppliers, Freeze-Dried Foods, Flour Mills, Food Storage, and Survival Products.

In addition, you might try any of the mail-order suppliers with whom I have personally worked and would recommend as reputable companies, as well as my own home storage business:

Peggy Layton
Food Storage Consultant
P.O. Box 44
Manti, UT 84642
Phone: (435) 835-0311
Fax: (435) 835-0312
E-mail: peggylayton@yahoo.com
Web site: www.peggylayton.com

Write or call for a current catalog and price list. I sell all the dehydrated food storage products talked about in this book: wheat grinders, bread mixers, emergency supplies, sun ovens, vital wheat gluten, metalized bucket liners, food dehydrators, sprouters, water purification, and much more. I also sell books on food storage and cooking, including four I authored and one I coauthored, and offer group discounts and wholesale prices for cookbooks. Available books include:

Cookin' with Home Storage, $16.95

Cookin' with Powdered Milk, $8.50

Cookin' with Dried Eggs, $6.50

Cookin' with Beans and Rice, $11.95

Cookin' with Kids in the Kitchen, $11.95

Shipping and handling charges are $ 3.75 for the first book and $.50 for each additional book. These additional titles will be available soon:

Cookin' with Dehydrated Food

Cookin' with Wheat and Other Grains

Cookin' with Dried Apples

Cookin' with Dried Potatoes

Copy Cat Cookin' (Make your own boxed mixes like Hamburger Helper, Rice-a-Roni, oatmeal packets, cakes, brownies, and a lot more.)

Great Grandmas' Recipes, Remedies, and Washday Hints

Get Out of Debt and Stay Out

I also offer personalized consulting services. That is, I will help you design a food storage program tailored for your family, assist you in finding the best prices available on products, and help you decide what you should and should not store. A well-planned-out food storage program in which you purchase only what is best for your family can save you hundreds of dollars.

Other Commercial Resources

The following are reputable mail-order companies that sell food storage and emergency supplies. Most of those included here have catalogs and Web sites with ordering information.

Bob's Red Mill
5209 S.E. International Way
Milwaukie, OR 97222
Phone: (503) 654-3215 or (800) 349-2173
Web site: www.bobsredmill.com

Grains, rice, kitchen equipment, hand and electric wheat grinders.

Christian Family Resources
P.O. Box 405
Kit Carson, CO 80825
Phone: (719) 962-3228
Web site: www.cfamilyresources.com

Dehydrated food and emergency supplies, water filters, grain mills, books.

Country Store
7704 N.E. 94th Avenue
Vancouver, WA 98674
Phone: (360) 891-4408 or (888) 311-8940
Web site: www.healthyharvest.com

Bosh Kitchen Appliance Center. Dehydrated food and emergency supplies.

Dottie's Kitchen Center
111 West Main Street
Puyallup, WA 98371

Phone: (253) 845-8003
Fax: (253) 845-8289
Web site: www.dottieskitchen.com

Dehydrated food, bread mixers, wheat grinders, kitchen supplies, and emergency supplies, books, grains, beans, and rice.

Emergency Essentials
362 South Commerce Loop
Orem, UT 84058
Phone: (800) 999-1863
Fax: (801) 222-9598
Web site: www.beprepared.com

Emergency survival equipment and supplies, freeze-dried backpacking food and supplies, food storage supplies, 72-hour kits, medical kits, car kits.

Frontier Survival
75 South Main Street
Manti, UT 84642
Phone: (435) 835-8698
Web site: www.frontiersurvival.com

Backpacking and camping supplies, 72-hour kits, Dutch ovens, emergency supplies, medical kits, tents, and fire-safety equipment.

General Supply
201 East Main
Farmington, NM 87401
Phone: (505) 325-7533
Fax: (800) 354-8896

Dehydrated food and emergency supplies.

Grandma's Country Foods
391 South Orange Street, Suite C
Salt Lake City, UT 84104
Phone: (801) 886-1110 or (800) 216-6466
Fax: (801) 886-3211
Web Site: www.grandmascountry.com

Bulk food storage products, spices, wheat grinders, and emergency equipment.

Honeyville Grain—Utah
635 North Billy Mitchell Road
Salt Lake City, UT 84116
Phone: (801) 972-2168 or (800) 280-2168
Web site: www.honeyvillegrain.com

White and red wheat, grains, oats, rice, and beans in bulk. Mixes, oil, shortening, dehydrated food.

Honeyville Grain—California
11600 Dayton Drive
Rancho Cucamonga, CA 91729
Phone: (909) 980-9500
Fax: (909) 980-6503
Web site: www.honeyvillegrain.com

White and red wheat, grains, oats, rice, and beans in bulk.

Lake Ridge Foods
896 East 640 North
Orem, UT 84097
Fax: (801) 221-8207

Dehydrated foods and emergency supplies.

LaRose Enterprise
3843 North 1000 West
Pleasant View, UT 84414
Phone: (801) 737-9475
E-mail: laroseenterprise@earthlink.net

Top-quality bulk spices, dehydrated foods, and restaurant supplies for home use.

Life Sprouts
P.O. Box 150
Hyrum, UT 84319
Phone: (800) 241-1516
Fax: (801) 245-3929
Web site: www.lifesprouts.com

Sprouting equipment, seeds, and books for all your sprouting needs.

Major Surplus and Supply
435 West Alondra Boulevard
Gardenia, CA 90248
Phone: (310) 324-8855 or (800) 441-8855
Fax: (310) 324-6909
Web site: www.majorsurplusnsurvival.com

Food storage supplies and emergency equipment.

The Maple Leaf Company
450 South 50 East
Ephraim, UT 84627
Phone: (435) 283-4400 or (800) 671-5323
Web site: www.mapleleafinc.com

Bulk food storage and dehydrated foods. Backpacking and camping equipment. Water barrels, spices, white and red wheat. Emergency supplies.

Nitro-Pak Preparedness Center
475 West 910 South Be Prepared Way
Heber City, UT 84032
Phone: (435) 654-0099 or (800) 866-4876
Web site: www.nitro-pak.com

Emergency supplies and equipment, food storage supplies, Mountain House freeze-dried foods, do-it-yourself canners, water filters, water barrels, 72-hour kits, and complete year's supply kits.

Preparedness Mart/Your Family Matters
1090 East Tabernacle Street
St. George, UT 84770
Phone: (435) 673-0437 or (800) 773-0437
Web site: www.preparednessmart.com

Dehydrated food and emergency supplies.

Preparedness Plus
P.O. Box 1985
Orem, UT 84059
Phone: (801) 226-4188 or (888) 839-0334
Fax: (801) 221-7449
Web site: www.preparednessplus.com

Dehydrated food, emergency supplies, solar ovens, and 72-hour kits.

New England Cheese Making Supply Company
P.O. Box 85
Ashfield, MA 01330

Phone: (413) 628-3808

Web site: www.cheesemaking.com

Starters for yogurt, buttermilk, and cheese. Cheese making supplies and equipment.

Ready Made Resources
239 Cagle Road
Tellico Plains, TN 37385
Phone: (423) 253-6789 or (800) 627-3809
Fax: (423) 253-2113
Web site: www.readymaderesources.com

Food storage and emergency supplies, kitchen equipment, military surplus, and gas masks.

Safari Sales
P.O. Box SS
Cortez, CO 81321
Phone: (800) 429-1856
Web site: www.survivalfoods.com

Dehydrated food and emergency survival equipment.

Yellowstone River Trading
P.O. Box 3235
Bozeman, MT 59772
Phone: (406) 586-8248 or (800) 585-5077
Fax: (406) 586-6398
Web sites: www.yellowstonetrading.com

Dehydrated food, emergency equipment, generators, and self-published book: *No Such Thing as Doomsday*.

INDEX

spoilage, power outages,
20–21
sprouting, steps to, 102–103
storage
action plan, 110–111
care needed, 65
containers, 72–74
debt avoidance, 48–50
deterioration/spoilage, causes,
68–70
deterioration/spoilage, preven-
tion, 70–72
family's needs and, 114
inventory taking, 125
meals/menus, 114
nutritional factors, 45–46
program planning, 109–110
quantity, 46–47
replenishing, 183
rotation system, 63–64, 67, 73
shelf life, 66–67
sprouts, 101
steps to, 111–113
taste factors, 46
variety, 75
waste, avoiding, 47–48
Freezing grain method, 72
French toast, 222
Fried rice, oriental, 245
Fruit
canned, 85
canning, 107
cocktail, 227
dehydrated, 85–87
freeze-dried, 87–88
salad, gelatin, 227

Fudge, pinto bean, 199
Fudge-flavored hot chocolate, 236
Fuel
alternative, 28–30
importance, 19
storage, 30

G

Gallon-can stove, 25–27
Garages, 57
Garbage bags, 74
Gardening, home
advantages, 94
composting, 99–100
grow boxes, 96–97
indoor, 98
locating plots, 94
seeds, 99
seeds, chart, 136–138
sprouting seeds, chart, 138
tools for, 94
Gelatin fruit salad, 227
Generators, 20
German pancakes, 224
Grains. *See also individual listings*
inventory list, 154–156
types, 81–82
Grandma's chicken noodle
soup, 255
Gravies, 80–81. *See also* Sauces
basic milk, 247
beef, 248
chicken, 247
herb, 249

T

Textured vegetable protein
(TVP)
about, 84–85
beef casserole, 262
beef and cheese macaroni, 265
beef stew, 263
chicken and noodles, 265
potato beef casserole, 263
sausage gravy over
biscuits, 264
tacos, 264
using, 261–262
veggie burgers, 266
Thermos wheat cereal, 211
Three bean salad, vinaigrette
style, 197
Toilets, 17–18
Tomatoes
beefy soup base, 251
juice, 250
paste, 249
sauce, 249
soup, 250
soup, cream of, 258
Tonic, wheatgrass, 103
Tortillas, whole wheat, 212
Traditional Italian minestrone
soup, 253
Trioxane, 30
TVP. *See* Textured vegetable
protein

U

Utilities. *See* Outages
Utility rooms, 57–59

V

Vegetables
canned, 85
canning, 106
dehydrated, 85–87
freeze-dried, 87–88
soup, creamy garden, 252
Veggie burgers, 266
Vermin, discouraging, 62–63

W

Waffles, crispy strawberry, 221
Water
after a disaster, 32
cloudy, 35
importance, 31
for pets, 89–90
purification devices, 35
storage
amount, 32–33
care needed, 65
checking on, 41
containers, 38–40
location, 37–38
sanitizing methods, 35–38
shelf-life, 40
types, 33
supplemental sources, 34
weight considerations, 8
Weevil infestation, 62
Wheat, steamed, 212
Wheatgrass tonic, 103
Whipped topping, home-
made, 234
White bread rolls, basic, 214

ABOUT THE AUTHOR

 Peggy Layton, a home economist, holds a bachelor's degree in home economics education from Brigham Young University, with a minor in food science and nutrition. Peggy and her husband, Scott, have seven children. With nine people to feed, Peggy writes about food storage and preparedness from a hands-on point of view. She writes and speaks frequently on bulk food preparation and emergency preparedness and has traveled extensively lecturing at preparedness expos throughout the United States. The author of a series of books on food storage and cooking, Peggy is also a food storage consultant and has helped many people put together food storage programs for their families. She is dedicated to bringing you accurate information as well as quality, tested recipes. Peggy and her family live in Manti, Utah, a rural town of 2,500 people, where they are prepared for any disaster—Peggy lives what she preaches!